Good Housekeeping

easy to make!
Smoothies
and Juices

COLLINS & BROWN

First published in Great Britain in 2009
by Collins & Brown
10 Southcombe Street
London W14 0RA

An imprint of Anova Books Company Ltd

The Good Housekeeping website is
www.allaboutyou.com/goodhousekeeping

1 2 3 4 5 6 7 8 9

ISBN 978-1-84340-496-5

A catalogue record for this book is available from the British
Library.

Reproduction by Dot Gradations Ltd
Printed by Times Offset, Malaysia

This book can be ordered direct from the publisher. Contact the
marketing department, but try your bookshop first.

www.anovabooks.com

NOTES

- Both metric and imperial measures are given for the recipes. Follow either set of measures, not a mixture of both, as they are not interchangeable.
- All spoon measures are level.
  1 tsp = 5ml spoon; 1 tbsp = 15ml spoon.
- Ovens and grills must be preheated to the specified temperature.
- Use sea salt and freshly ground black pepper unless otherwise suggested.
- Fresh herbs should be used unless dried herbs are specified in a recipe.
- Medium eggs should be used except where otherwise specified. Free-range eggs are recommended.
- Note that certain recipes contain raw or lightly cooked eggs. The young, elderly, pregnant women and anyone with an immune-deficiency disease should avoid these, because of the slight risk of salmonella.
- Calorie, fat and carbohydrate counts per serving are provided for the recipes.

Picture credits
Photographers: Nicki Dowey
Craig Robertson (Basics section, apart from pages 10, 12, 13, Nicki Dowey)
Lucinda Symons (page 64)
Will Heap (page 69)

Contents

Foreword

With so many gorgeous ingredients available in the shops now, it's easy to make smoothies and juices at home. Any combination of fruits blended together will taste good. Just throw it all in a blender, add yogurt or milk if you like it creamy, or oats to add give body, and whizz until everything comes together. They're perfect for breakfast as they're so filling and good for using up fruit that's ripened a little too quickly in the bowl. It's not just fruit that can play a starring role ... veg works just as well. The roots, such as carrot or beetroot, will add earthy sweetness, while cucumber, with its high water content will give it a fresh savoury note. Add ice and you'll have a chilled drink that will instantly cool you down on a hot summer's day.

This book has everything you need for making delicious drinks. There are recipes ideal for breakfast – try Carrot With a Bite on page 66 or Mango and Oat Smoothie on page 68. If you're throwing a party, flick to page 108, where there are plenty of ideas to inspire you. We've also included handy tips on buying the right equipment and cleaning it properly to help ensure it continues to work well. All the recipes have been triple tested in the Good Housekeeping kitchens to make sure they work every time for you.

Enjoy,

Emma

Emma Marsden
Cookery Editor
Good Housekeeping

0

The Basics

Fruit and vegetables

One of the easiest ways to stay healthy is to eat plenty of fruit and vegetables. They contain an arsenal of vitamins, minerals, fibre and phytochemicals – which is why nutrition experts believe that they are the cornerstone of a healthy diet.

Different coloured fruit and vegetables contain a variety of vitamins, minerals and phytochemicals that help to keep you healthy in different ways, and so to make sure you get a good intake of all these nutrients you need to eat an array of produce.

You probably already know that you should be eating at least five servings of fruit and vegetables a day, but did you know you should also be eating a rainbow? Think of red, orange, yellow, green and purple fruit and vegetables and aim for at least one serving from each of the colour bands every day.

Fresh or frozen?

Most of the recipes in this book call for fresh fruits, but frozen fruit make excellent smoothies, too. Berries can be frozen whole; tropical fruit such as mangoes or pineapples can also be frozen, chopped into bite-sized pieces. You can use them from frozen or thawed; if you thaw them, remember to use the juice, too.

Canned fruit in natural juice is a good standby, and dried fruit such as apricots and prunes provide sweetness, fibre and certain nutrients. Soak dried fruit before blending or use ready-to-eat dried fruit.

An easy way to five a day

Smoothies and juices are a great way of increasing your fruit, vegetable and fluid intake. The term 'smoothie' refers to drinks made in a blender: they can be sweet or savoury, solely from fruit and vegetables, or blended with added dairy or non-dairy ingredients. Making your own smoothies means you know exactly what's in them. Home-made smoothies are deliciously varied and can make good nutritional sense for all of us.

Vitamins and minerals

Vitamins

Our bodies cannot make all the vitamins we need, so we need to get them from our food and drink. They are vital to good health and effective in very small amounts.

Vitamin A – needed for growth and development, healthy eyesight and good skin. Yellow, orange and green fruit and vegetables are rich in the antioxidant beta-carotene, which the body converts into vitamin A.

Vitamin B complex: B1 (thiamin), B2 (riboflavin, B3 (niacin), B6 (pyridoxine), B12 (cobalamin), biotin, pantothenic acid, folic acid - these vitamins work together to help digestion and aid resistance to infection. Whole grains are rich in these vitamins, as are sprouting seeds, green vegetables and citrus fruits.

Vitamin C – an antioxidant which protects the bones, joints, teeth, gums, nerves, glands and other tissues and aids the absorption of iron. Found in varying amounts in all fresh fruits and vegetables.

Vitamin E – an antioxidant held in cell membranes that is essential for normal metabolism, aids heart function and may protect against heart disease. Found mainly in whole grains, seeds, nuts and green vegetables.

Minerals

These are needed in tiny quantities and are far more readily absorbed by the body than those from supplements. Some of the more important minerals are calcium (for healthy teeth and bones), iron (helps transport oxygen in the blood), magnesium, zinc, potassium, phosphorous, sulphur and selenium.

Antioxidants

Some vitamins and minerals are antioxidants: they can reduce the risk of many diseases by protecting cells against 'free radicals' which maybe harmful.

Fibre

Don't forget fibre in your diet; it is vitally important for good digestion. Fruit smoothies are an excellent fibre source: blended fruit and vegetables retain their fibre, although much is lost when they are juiced. You can add extra fibre to smoothies in the form of oats and sprouting seeds, but if your diet contains other sources of fibre such as pulses and whole grains, this is not necessary.

Sugar

Too much sugar in the diet is a major cause of tooth decay and can lead to obesity, with all the associated health risks. Fruit and vegetables contain varying amounts of a natural sugar called fructose; you will soon get used to the natural sweetness of fruit and vegetables. If you do find it necessary to add a little more sweetness, then choose honey or maple syrup, A word of warning: drinking too much fruit juice can give your system an overload of sugar, so if you suffer from sugar intolerance (hypoglycaemia), diabetes or Candidiasis (yeast infections and thrush), you should be wary of the amount you consume; check recommended intakes with your GP.

Fat

A small amount of fat in the diet is vital for good health: the essential fatty acids (EFAs) found in nuts and seeds as well as in olive oil and oily fish and in smaller amounts in other foods are needed for healthy heart and brain function. However, too much fat will lead to weight gain and an increased risk of heart disease. Most fruit smoothies are low in fat.

Dairy produce from animal sources is a rich source of calcium, but many milkshakes and yogurt drinks are high in less-healthy saturated fats. Keep the intake of these fats to a minimum and try using non-dairy products such as calcium-enriched soya milk and oat milk instead.

Blenders

A blender is designed to liquidise or 'pulp' whatever is put into it by 'shredding' at a high speed. Free-standing 'jug' blenders have a large removable jug made from glass or sturdy plastic, with metal blades, set on a motor with variable speeds – more expensive models have a blade which is strong enough to crush ice. Never assume that your blender can crush ice, always check the manufacturer's information, otherwise you may seriously damage the motor.

Some food processors and mixers have a blender attachment, which fits alongside or on top of the main processing bowl. There are also smaller hand-held blenders which either come with a small canister or bowl, or can be used with your own jug or container. It's worth investigating how the bits and pieces come apart for ease of cleaning and maintenance, and check the parts are dishwasher-safe.

Juice extractors

Not all fruit and vegetables are suitable for blending. Harder textured ones like apples and carrots will pulverise but not soften completely as they are more fibrous. So if you want to have a wider choice, with maximum nutritional benefit, then perhaps you should think about using a juicer to make your own juices. There are three different types of machine for juice extraction:

Centrifugal – reasonably priced, electrically powered, high-speed juicer that shreds up fruit and vegetables, and then spins the pulp at high speed in a meshed basket, separating out the juice into a jug, while the pulp stays in the basket. This type of juicer needs thorough cleaning after each use. Check it is dishwasher-safe as parts can be time-consuming to wash by hand.
Masticating – more expensive and works at a slower speed than a centrifugal juicer. It chews up fruit and vegetables into a paste and then squeezes the juice through a mesh at the bottom, leaving a dry pulp. This type copes well with skin, peel and pips.

Equipment

Making your own smoothies can easily become part of your daily routine. All you need to get started is a blender; then, if you really get into smoothie-making, it's worth investing in a juice extractor, so you can enjoy the maximum benefit from readily available ingredients such as apples and carrots.

Slow-turning or wheatgrass juicer – operates in a very different manner from high-speed juicers. A motor slowly turns a blade inside the juicer which presses juices from leafy greens, sprouts, wheatgrass and soft vegetables, rather than masticating them.

What to look for in a juicer:

A large feed chute cuts down on preparation time. Some can take whole apples.
A removable pulp-collecting container. To make emptying less messy, put a plastic bag inside the container; when it is full, pop the bag in the bin.
A 1 litre (1³/₄ pint) juice jug.

Maintenance

Always keep your drink-making equipment clean and dry to avoid contamination. If you have been using strongly flavoured ingredients, make sure you rinse out the container thoroughly so that these flavours don't taint future drinks. Some juices such as carrot or beetroot may cause discolouration, but this will not affect the performance of the appliance. Some discolouration can be removed by rubbing with a cloth dipped in vegetable oil.

No equipment? No problem

If you don't have a blender or food processor, then you can simply mash ripe fruit like bananas, mangoes or avocados with a fork. Certain types of fruit such as berries and fresh currants can be rubbed through a fine-mesh sieve.

If time is short and you just want to get started, there is a wide selection of ready-prepared organic and non-organic juices on the market, from the shelf and chiller cabinet. But don't forget that even 100% juice has been processed to a point that most of the vitamins and minerals listed on the label are additives, and ready-made juices are more expensive than buying the raw ingredients.

Citrus juicers

These extract juice from all citrus fruit. There are several types of manual juicers, or they can be electric – halved fruit is held on a rotating cone causing the juice to fall into a container below The resulting juice is clearer and thinner than juice made in other types of juicer. These are easier to clean because there are no grating teeth to trap fruit residue.

Healthy ingredients

Food	Choose	Nutrition	Benefits
Apple	Firm, crisp, flavoursome apples. Peel and core for blending or juice the whole fruit.	Useful supply of beta-carotene, vitamins B1, B2, B6, C, biotin and folic acid, and minerals calcium, potassium, magnesium and phosphorus.	The malic acid and tartaric acid content help relieve indigestion, and help break down fatty foods and too much protein. An excellent appetite quencher if you're on a slimming diet.
Apricot	Ripe, unblemished, golden-orange fruit. Wash well, halve and stone before using.	Excellent supply of beta-carotene; useful amounts of vitamins C, B3, folic acid and pantothenic acid, and minerals potassium, calcium, magnesium, sulphur and phosphorus.	Owing to the high beta-carotene content, apricots are excellent for fighting infection, especially of the respiratory system.
Avocado	Ripe fruit, which gives slightly when lightly squeezed. Peel and stone before blending. Add lemon juice to prevent discolouration.	A high-fat fruit with useful amounts of beta-carotene, vitamins C and E, and smaller amounts of the B complex; rich in potassium, with good supplies of calcium, magnesium, phosphorus, zinc and sulphur.	An excellent fruit for a high-energy drink.
Banana	Ripe, yellow fruit. Simply peel and blend or mash, then mix with other juices or ingredients.	Good supply of beta-carotene, and useful amounts of vitamins E, B3, folic acid, biotin and C. A rich supply of potassium, and a good supply of magnesium, phosphorus, sulphur and chlorine.	Easily digested when ripe, bananas are an excellent fruit to aid digestion and for convalescence. The rich potassium supply gives a real boost to our body's maintenance programme.
Beetroot	Cooked, peeled baby beetroot in natural juice – usually available vacuum packed.	High in folic acid, with smaller amounts of beta-carotene, vitamins B1, B2, B3, pantothenic acid and C. Contains an abundance of minerals: high in potassium, sodium, calcium, phosphorus, iron and chlorine.	A powerful cleanser and tonic, particularly beneficial to the liver. A good aid to recovery during convalescence.
Blackcurrant	Organic fresh or frozen fruits. Wash well and strip the fruit from the stalks, then blend whole.	Rich in beta-carotene and vitamin C, with smaller amounts of B3, pantothenic acid, biotin, and E. High in potassium and calcium, with good supplies of magnesium, phosphorus, iron, sulphur and chlorine.	The skins contain compounds that have the ability to inhibit the growth of harmful bacteria. The high vitamin C content gives blackcurrants powerful antioxidant properties.
Blueberry	Ripe, unblemished fruit. Use fresh or frozen. Wash well and use whole.	Useful supplies of beta-carotene, the B complex and C vitamins; and a good supply of potassium and calcium. Also provides magnesium, phosphorus, sulphur and chlorine.	The skins contain high concentrations of compounds that can destroy harmful bacteria in the gut and keep it healthy.

Food	Choose	Nutrition	Benefits
Carrot	Firm carrots with a deep even orange colour. No spade marks or disease. Scrub well or peel, remove tops and chop before juicing.	Extremely high beta-carotene content, with useful quantities of vitamins B1, B3, B6, folic acid and pantothenic acid. Carrots also contain small amounts of sodium, potassium, calcium, phosphorus, iron, sulphur and chlorine.	An excellent tonic and rejuvenator. Stimulates the digestion and is a mild diuretic.
Celery	Firm and crisp stalks; no wilting or damage. Wash well, trim and chop before using.	Useful amounts of beta-carotene, vitamins B3, folic acid, pantothenic acid, biotin and E. Rich in potassium, calcium and chlorine.	Has a calming effect on the nervous system; helps to eliminate waste from the kidneys.
Cherry	Deep, dark-coloured, ripe cherries that are firm to the touch. Time-consuming as they must be washed, destalked and stoned.	A good source of beta-carotene and vitamin C, plus useful amounts of B3, folic acid and biotin; and minerals potassium, calcium, magnesium, phosphorus and sulphur.	A very alkaline juice, which can reduce the acidity of the blood, so it is very effective for the treatment of gout and arthritis.
Cranberry	Deep-coloured firm fruit, fresh or frozen. Wash well before using.	Good source of beta-carotene, B complex vitamins, folic acid and C, and minerals potassium, calcium, magnesium, phosphorus, iron and sulphur.	A natural diuretic and urinary tract cleanser. Cranberries increase the urine's acidity and thus destroy bacteria; useful in the treatment of cystitis.
Cucumber	Unwaxed, firm, dark green medium length cucumbers. Peel cucumbers that are waxed; otherwise wash well, trim and chop.	Useful amounts of beta-carotene – note: most is in the cucumber skin - vitamins B3, folic acid, pantothenic acid, biotin, potassium, calcium, phosphorus, iron, sulphur and chlorine.	Natural diuretic; good for skin rejuvenation.
Grape	Any sweet variety of grape can be used, as long as they are fresh and firm. Simply wash well, pull out the stalks and use – seeds can be left in if liked.	Good supply of beta-carotene, vitamins B3, B6, folic acid, biotin and C; and minerals potassium, calcium, magnesium, phosphorus and sulphur.	An excellent metabolism stimulator and blood cleanser; good for convalescence to promote a feeling of well-being. Grapes are best taken on their own because they ferment quickly in the stomach if held back by other foods.
Grapefruit	Heavy fruits with thin skin. Pink and Ruby grapefruits are sweeter and less acidic than white varieties. Peel, remove as much white pith as possible, quarter and discard the pips.	Pink varieties are rich in beta-carotene, but all are rich in vitamin C and folic acid, potassium, calcium, magnesium, phosphorus, sulphur and chlorine.	A beneficial juice for improving the skin.

Food	Choose	Nutrition	Benefits
Kiwi Fruit	Firm, unblemished fruit. Peel away the skin and cut into quarters before blending.	Excellent source of vitamin C and a good source of beta-carotene; and minerals potassium, calcium, magnesium, phosphorus, sulphur and chlorine.	Good for circulation, digestion and the skin; can help lift depression by giving your system a boost.
Lemon (and Lime)	Firm fruit with thin skins. Peel away the skin and as much white pith as possible; chop and remove the pips.	High in vitamin C, with a smaller supply of beta-carotene, vitamins B1, B2, B3, B6 and pantothenic acid; and minerals potassium, calcium, magnesium, phosphorus and iron. Limes have a slightly lower nutritional content.	Lemons are well known as a cure for scurvy – a disease caused by a diet deficient in vitamin C. They are also used as a remedy for colds and sore throats. Juice is a good cleanser when drunk in small amounts before a meal and an effective antioxidant. When added to other fruit and vegetables, it can prevent discolouration and acts as a mild preservative. Limes are less acidic.
Mango	Firm fruits, which give slightly when gently squeezed. Peel and slice the flesh away from the stone, and skin, and then blend.	Very high in beta-carotene, with a good supply of vitamin C, and smaller amounts of B1, B2, B3 and E. It also has a good supply of potassium, calcium, magnesium, phosphorus and iron.	An excellent fruit for energy and vitality, and promoting healthy skin.
Melon (Yellow and Orange varieties)	Firm melons with a 'sweet' smell. A heavy melon will be more juicy. Halve or slice, remove seeds and skin before blending.	Cantaloupe and other orange-fleshed melons are high in beta-carotene. Useful supply of the B complex and a little vitamin C. Good supply of potassium, calcium, magnesium, phosphorus and chlorine.	A calming effect on the digestive system, with a mild stimulating action on the kidneys and a gentle laxative effect.
Orange	Firm, heavy juicing oranges with thin skins. Peel away the skin and white pith; chop and remove the pips.	Blood oranges have the highest amount of beta-carotene; all oranges are rich in vitamin C and folic acid. There are smaller amounts of B1, B2, B3, B6, pantothenic acid and E. Good supply of potassium, calcium, magnesium, phosphorus, sulphur and chlorine.	As with other citrus juices, oranges help to cleanse and improve the digestive system. Cells, capillaries, heart and lungs benefit from orange juice, and it is also good for maintaining healthy skin.
Papaya (Paw Paw)	A golden yellow skin denotes ripeness. Fruits should give a little when lightly squeezed. Peel, cut in half and scoop out the seeds, then blend.	High in beta-carotene and vitamin C, with a useful supply of the B complex, potassium, calcium, magnesium, phosphorus, sulphur and chlorine.	Contains several enzymes, principally papain, which aids the digestion of protein. It is a real energy booster; it helps stimulate the appetite; it has a mild laxative effect and is a good cleanser for the internal organs.

Food	Choose	Nutrition	Benefits
Peach (and Nectarine)	Deep-coloured fruits that give a little when gently pressed. Wash well, halve and remove the stone before blending.	Peaches and nectarines are very similar nutritionally. They have a good supply of beta-carotene and vitamin C, with useful quantities of the B complex. Minerals include potassium, calcium, magnesium, phosphorus, iron and sulphur.	Cleansing to the intestine and stimulates bowel movements.
Pear	Look for rich-coloured, firm, unblemished fruit. Peel and remove core and seeds before blending.	All varieties contain beta-carotene, vitamins B1, B2, B3, B6, folic acid and biotin, and C; and minerals potassium, calcium, magnesium, phosphorus, iron and sulphur.	Mild diuretic and laxative.
Pineapple	A golden skin, a prominent 'sweet' smell, flesh that gives a little when pressed. When pineapple is ripe, a leaf can easily be pulled from its crown.	Good supply of vitamin C, and smaller amounts of beta-carotene and the B complex vitamins. Rich in potassium and chlorine, with smaller amounts of calcium, magnesium, phosphorus and sulphur.	Contains enzyme bromelain, which aids the digestion of protein, and therefore is excellent for digestive problems.
Raspberry	Ripe, firm, unbruised fruits. Wash well, remove the stalks before blending. Use fresh or frozen for smoothies.	Good supply of vitamin C and folic acid with smaller amounts of beta-carotene, B1, B2, B3, B6, pantothenic acid and E. Raspberries contain potassium, calcium, magnesium, phosphorus, iron, zinc, sulphur and chlorine.	Excellent uplifting properties and good for convalescence. Also have healing properties for the digestive tract.
Strawberry	Ripe, sweet-smelling, unblemished fruit. Wash well. Remove the stalks and hulls before blending.	Rich in vitamin C and folic acid; also contains beta-carotene, B1, B2, B3, B6, pantothenic acid and biotin. Rich in potassium, calcium, magnesium, phosphorus, sulphur and chlorine.	A good cleanser for the whole body and a mild diuretic.
Tomato	Vine-ripened, red tomatoes. Wash well and remove stalks before blending.	High in beta-carotene with good amounts of vitamins B3, folic acid, C and E. Also good supply of potassium, iron, chlorine.	Stimulates circulation and contains the potentially cancer-fighting compound lycopene.
Watermelon	Well-rounded fruit with a smooth, hard skin. Remove the skin and seeds before blending.	Rich in beta-carotene with useful amounts of vitamins B1, B2, B3, B6, folic acid, pantothenic acid, biotin and C, and minerals potassium, calcium, magnesium, phosphorus and iron.	An excellent cleanser for the bladder and kidneys; it is a mild diuretic, and is a natural appetite stimulator.

Extra boosts

There are many ingredients that you can add to smoothies if you have specific nutritional requirements.

Acidophilus

A probiotic: 'friendly' bacteria that promote good health. Acidophilus is most beneficial when taken if you are suffering from diarrhoea or after a course of antibiotics, or if you have digestive problems such as irritable bowel syndrome (IBS). Available from most chemists and health shops in capsule form, which usually need to be kept in the refrigerator. Probiotics are now included in some ready-made drinks and yogurt products.

Bee pollen

A natural antibiotic and a source of antioxidants, bee pollen is a good general tonic. It contains plenty of protein and essential amino acids. Available as loose powder, granules or in tablet or capsule form.
Warning: it can cause an allergic reaction in pollen-sensitive individuals.

Brewers' yeast

A by-product of beer brewing, brewers' yeast is exceptionally rich in B vitamins, with high levels of iron, zinc, magnesium and potassium. Highly concentrated and an excellent pick-me-up, but the flavour is strong and needs to be mixed with other ingredients. Available as pills or powder.
Warning: it is high in purines so should be avoided by gout sufferers.

Echinacea

Recommended by herbalists for many years, echinacea is a native plant of North America, taken to support a healthy immune system. A great all-rounder with anti-viral and anti-bacterial properties. Comes in capsules and in extracts taken in drops, so is easy to add to smoothies.
Warning: not recommended for use during pregnancy or when breastfeeding.

Eggs

High in protein, but eggs also contain cholesterol so you might need to limit your intake; ask your GP. Egg white powder is low in fat and can be added to smoothies for a protein boost. Always use the freshest eggs for smoothies.
Warning: raw egg should not be eaten by the elderly, children, babies, pregnant women or those with an impaired immune system as there can be a risk of contracting salmonella.

Ginseng

Derived from the roots of a plant grown in Russia, Korea and China. The active constituents are ginsenosides, reputed to stimulate the hormones and increase energy. Available in dry root form for grinding or ready powdered. **Warning:** should not be taken by those suffering from hypertension.

Nuts

Packed with nutrients, nuts are a concentrated form of protein and are rich in antioxidants, vitamins B1, B6 and E, and many minerals. Brazil nuts are one of the best sources of selenium in the diet. Nuts do have a high fat content, but this is mostly unsaturated fat. Walnuts are particularly high in omega-3, an essential fatty acid that is needed for healthy heart and brain function. Brazil, cashew, coconut, peanut and macadamia nuts contain more saturated fat, so should be used sparingly. Almonds are particularly easy to digest. Finely chop or grind the nuts just before using for maximum freshness.

Seeds

Highly nutritious, seeds contain a good supply of essential fatty acids (EFAs). Flaxseed (linseed) is particularly beneficial as it is one of the richest sources of omega-3 EFAs, with 57% more than oily fish. Pumpkin, sesame and sunflower seeds also work well in smoothies. They are best bought in small amounts as their fat content makes them go rancid quickly, so store in airtight containers in the refrigerator. Grind them just before use for maximum benefit, or use the oils – these have to be stored in the refrigerator.

Sprouting seeds

These are simply seeds from a variety of plants – such as sunflower, chickpea and mung bean – which have been given a little water and warmth and have started to grow. Sprouts are full of vitamins, minerals, proteins and carbohydrates. They are pretty soft so they whiz up easily in the blender for savoury smoothies.

Oats

Sold in the form of whole grain, rolled, flaked or ground (oatmeal), oats are high in protein, vitamin B complex, vitamin E, potassium, calcium, phosphorus, iron and zinc; they are easy to digest and can soothe the digestive tract. They are also a rich source of soluble fibre, which helps to lower high blood cholesterol levels, which in turn will help reduce the risk of heart disease. Toasted oatmeal has a nutty flavour and is ideal for smoothies. **Warning:** oats should be avoided by those on a gluten-free diet.

Wheat bran and germ

Wheat bran is the outside of the wheat grain removed during milling; it is very high in fibre and adds bulk to the diet. It is bland in taste but adds a crunchy texture. Wheat germ, from the centre of the grain, is very nutritious and easy to digest, with a mild flavour. Highly perishable, store in the refrigerator once the pack is opened. **Warning:** keep your intake of bran to moderate levels; large amounts can prevent vitamins and minerals from being absorbed.

Non-dairy alternatives

Soya milk and yogurt

If you are allergic to dairy products or lactose-intolerant, drinking milk may cause a variety of symptoms, including skin rashes and eczema, asthma and irritable bowel syndrome. Soya milk and yogurt are useful alternatives – look for calcium-enriched products. Good non-dairy sources of calcium suitable for adding to smoothies include dark green leafy vegetables, such as watercress and spinach, and apricots.

Silken tofu

This protein-rich dairy-free product adds a creamy texture to fruit and vegetable smoothies.

Apples

1 To core an apple, push an apple corer straight through the apple from the stem to the base. Remove the core and use a small sharp knife to pick out any stray seeds or seed casings.

2 To peel, hold the fruit in one hand and run a swivel peeler under the skin, starting from the stem end and moving around the fruit, taking off the skin until you reach the base.

Preparing fruit

A few simple techniques can make preparing fruit quick and easy.

Pears

1 To core, use a teaspoon to scoop out the seeds and core through the base of the pear. Trim away any remaining fragments with a small knife. If you halve or quarter the pear, remove any remaining seeds.

2 To peel, cut off the stem. Peel off the skin in even strips from tip to base. If not using immediately, toss the pears in lemon juice.

Preserving colour

The flesh of apples, pears and other fruit starts to turn brown when exposed to air. If you are not going to use the prepared fruit immediately, toss with lemon juice.

Peaches, nectarines, plums and apricots

Really ripe fruit can be very soft, so handle with care.

Removing the stones

1 Following the cleft along one side of the fruit, cut through to the stone all around the fruit.

2 Twist gently to separate the halves. Ease out the stone with a small knife. If you are not using immediately, rub the flesh with lemon juice.

Peeling peaches

1 To remove the fuzzy skin from peaches, put in a bowl of boiling water for 15 seconds–1 minute (depending on ripeness). Don't leave in the water for too long, as heat will soften the flesh. Put in cold water.

2 Work a knife between the skin and flesh to loosen the skin, then gently pull to remove. Rub the flesh with lemon juice.

Cherries

For use in smoothies, cherries need to be stoned, or pitted. A cherry stoner will do this neatly, but it is important to position the fruit correctly on the cherry stoner.

1 First, remove the stems from the cherries, and then wash the fruits and pat dry on kitchen paper.

2 Put each cherry on the stoner with the stem end facing up. Close the stoner and gently press the handles together so that the metal rod pushes through the fruit, pressing out the stone.

3 Alternatively, if you do not have a cherry stoner, cut the cherries in half and remove the stones with the tip of a small, pointed knife.

Hulling strawberries

1 Wash the strawberries gently and dry on kitchen paper. Remove the hull (the centre part that was attached to the plant) from the strawberry using a strawberry huller or a small sharp knife.

2 Put the knife into the small, hard area beneath the green stalk and gently rotate to remove a small, cone-shaped piece.

Berries

Soft fruits - strawberries, blackberries, raspberries and currants - are generally quick to prepare. Always handle ripe fruits gently as they can bruise easily .

Washing berries

Most soft fruits can be washed very gently in cold water. Shop-bought blackberries will usually have the hull removed. If you have picked blackberries yourself the hulls and stalks may still be attached, so pick over the berries carefully and remove any that remain. Carefully remove any stalks and hulls from raspberries. Leave strawberries whole.

1 Place the berries in a bowl of cold water and allow any small pieces of grit, dust or insects to float out.

2 Transfer the fruit to a colander and rinse gently under fresh running water. Drain well, then leave to drain on kitchen paper.

Currants

Blackcurrants, redcurrants and whitecurrants can all be stripped quickly from the stem in the same way.

1 Using a fork, strip all the currants off the stalks by running the fork down the length of the stalk.

2 Put the currants into a colander and wash them gently.

Melons

1 Halve the melon by cutting horizontally through the middle.

2 Use a spoon to scoop out the seeds and fibres, and pull or cut out any that remain. Cut off the skin using a sharp knife.

Watermelons

Slice the watermelons into wedges and use a small teaspoon or small pointed knife to pick out the seeds.

Ginger

Ginger makes a great addition to smoothies based on melons, apples and carrots.

1 Peel fresh root ginger with a vegetable peeler and cut off any soft brown spots. Chop roughly.

2 **Pressing** If you need to use the juice and don't have a blender, cut thick slices off the ginger root, and remove the skin and any soft brown spots. Cut the slices into chunks, and press them with a garlic press into a small bowl.

Citrus fruit

Using a sharp knife, cut off the peel from the whole fruit, removing as much of the white pith as possible. Chop the flesh roughly, discarding any pips.

Pineapples

1 Cut off the base and crown of the pineapple, and stand the fruit on a chopping board.

2 Using a medium-sized knife, peel away a section of skin going just deep enough to remove all or most of the hard, inedible 'eyes' on the skin. Repeat all the way around.

3 Use a small knife to cut out any remaining traces of the eyes.

4 Cut the peeled pineapple into slices, or chop roughly.

Mangoes

This is an effective way to remove as much flesh as possible without too much mess.

1 Cut a slice to one side of the stone in centre. Repeat on the other side.

2 Cut parallel lines into the flesh of one slice, almost to the skin. Cut another set of lines to cut the flesh into squares.

3 Press on the skin side to turn the fruit inside out, so that the flesh is thrust outwards. Cut off the chunks as close as possible to the skin. Repeat with the other half.

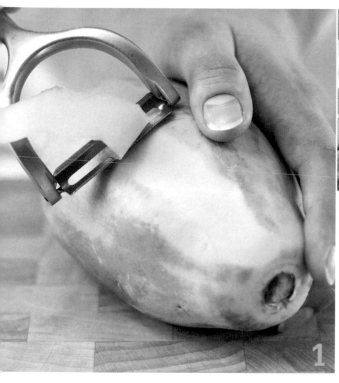

Papaya

1 Peel the fruit using a swivel-headed vegetable peeler, then gently cut in half using a sharp knife.

2 Use a teaspoon to scoop out the shiny black seeds and fibres inside the cavity. Chop the flesh roughly.

Passion fruit

1 The seeds are edible, or can be sieved out. Halve the passion fruit and scoop the seeds and pulp into a food processor or blender. Process for 30 seconds, until the mixture looks soupy.

2 Pour into a sieve over a bowl, and press down hard with the back of a spoon to release the juice.

Seeding tomatoes

1 Halve the tomato through the core. Use a spoon or a small sharp knife to remove the seeds and juice. Shake off the excess liquid.

2 Chop the tomato as required for your recipe and place in a colander for a minute or two, to drain off any excess liquid.

Watercress and spinach

These need to be washed thoroughly before adding to smoothies. Immerse in a bowl of cold water for a few minutes and swirl the leaves to loosen any dirt. Repeat if necessary. Lift out and place in a colander, rinse under the cold tap, leave to drain for a few minutes, then shake off excess water.

Preparing vegetables

Packed with vitamins and minerals and low in calories, vegetables are a nutritious ingredient of many smoothies.

Perfect herbs

- Parsley, mint and coriander are ideal to add flavour to savoury smoothies.
- Trim off the roots and the fleshy part of the stalks (parsley and coriander stalks can be saved to flavour stock or soup).
- Immerse the herbs in cold water for a few minutes, lift out and place in a colander. Rinse under the cold tap, leave to drain briefly, then shake off excess water.

Avocados

Prepare avocados just before serving because their flesh discolours quickly once exposed to air.

1 Halve the avocado lengthways and twist the two halves apart. Tap the stone with a sharp knife, then twist to remove the stone.

2 Run a knife between the flesh and skin and pull away. Slice the flesh.

Carrots

Carrot juice is naturally sweet and is good mixed with other vegetable juices.

1 Cut off the ends and peel off the skin using a vegetable peeler.

2 Cut lengthways (depending on the size of the carrot), then chop across the width.

Celery

1 To remove the strings, trim the ends and cut through the base to separate the stalks. Set aside the inner stalks.

2 Cut into the base of the green outer stalks with a small knife and catch the strings between the blade and your thumb. Pull up towards the top of the stalk to remove the strings

Beetroot

When you are peeling or preparing raw beetroot, wear rubber gloves and work over a plate rather than a chopping board, as the beetroot colour will stain your hands and the board. Be careful of your clothing, too, as the juice can stain.

Hygiene

When you are preparing food, always follow these important guidelines:

Wash your hands thoroughly before handling food and again between handling different types of food, such as eggs and cream. If you have any cuts or grazes on your hands, be sure to keep them covered with a waterproof plaster.

Wash down worksurfaces regularly with a mild detergent solution or multi-surface cleaner.

Use a dishwasher if available. Otherwise, wear rubber gloves for washing-up, so that the water temperature can be hotter than unprotected hands can bear. Change drying-up cloths and cleaning cloths regularly. Note that leaving dishes to drain is more hygienic than drying them with a teatowel.

Keep raw and cooked foods separate. Wash kitchen utensils in between preparing raw and cooked foods. Never put cooked or ready-to-eat foods directly on to a surface which has just had raw fish, meat or poultry on it.

Keep pets out of the kitchen if possible; or make sure they stay away from worksurfaces. Never allow animals on to worksurfaces.

Food storage and hygiene

Storing food properly and preparing it in a hygienic way is important to ensure that food remains as nutritious and flavourful as possible, and to reduce the risk of food poisoning.

Shopping

Always choose fresh ingredients in prime condition from stores and markets that have a regular turnover of stock to ensure you buy the freshest produce possible.

Avoid damaged, bruised or wilting produce, and remember that fruit and vegetables begin to lose vitamin C after they are picked.

Make sure produce is fully ripe, as it will be easier to digest.

Make sure items are within their 'best before' or 'use by' date. (Foods with a longer shelf life have a 'best before' date; more perishable items have a 'use by' date.)

Pack frozen and chilled items in an insulated cool bag at the check-out and put them into the freezer or refrigerator as soon as you get home.

During warm weather in particular, buy perishable foods just before you return home. When packing items at the check-out, sort them according to where you will store them when you get home – the refrigerator, freezer, storecupboard, vegetable rack, fruit bowl, etc. This will make unpacking easier – and quicker.

The storecupboard

Although storecupboard ingredients will generally last a long time, correct storage is important:

Always check packaging for storage advice – even with familiar foods, because storage requirements may change if additives, sugar or salt have been reduced. Check storecupboard foods for their 'best before' or 'use by' date and do not use them if the date has passed.

Keep all food cupboards scrupulously clean and make sure food containers and packets are properly sealed.

Once opened, treat canned foods as though fresh. Always transfer the contents to a clean container, cover and keep in the refrigerator. Similarly, jars, sauce bottles and cartons should be kept chilled after opening. (Check the label for safe storage times after opening.)

Store dry goods such as sugar in airtight, moisture-proof containers. When supplies are used up, wash the container well and thoroughly dry before refilling with new supplies.

Store dried herbs, spices and flavourings in a cool, dark cupboard or in dark jars. Buy in small quantities as their flavour will not last indefinitely.

Refrigerator storage

Fresh food needs to be kept in the cool temperature of the refrigerator to keep it in good condition and discourage the growth of harmful bacteria. Store day-to-day perishable items, such as opened jams and jellies in the refrigerator along with eggs and dairy products, fruit juices, salads and vegetables. A refrigerator should be kept at an operating temperature of 4–5°C. It is worth investing in a refrigerator thermometer to ensure the correct temperature is maintained.

To ensure your refrigerator is functioning effectively for safe food storage, follow these guidelines:

To avoid bacterial cross-contamination, store cooked and raw foods on separate shelves, putting cooked foods on the top shelf. Ensure that all items are well wrapped.

Never put hot food into the refrigerator, as this will cause the internal temperature of the refrigerator to rise.

Avoid overfilling the refrigerator, as this restricts the circulation of air and prevents the appliance from working properly.

It can take some time for the refrigerator to return to the correct operating temperature once the door has been opened, so don't leave it open any longer than is necessary.

Clean the refrigerator regularly, using a specially formulated germicidal refrigerator cleaner. Alternatively, use a weak solution of bicarbonate of soda: 1 tbsp to 1 litre (1³/₄ pints) water.

If your refrigerator doesn't have an automatic defrost facility, defrost regularly.

Maximum refrigerator storage times

The following storage times should apply, providing the food is in prime condition when it goes into the refrigerator and the appliance is in good working order:

Fruit

Hard and stone fruit	3–7 days
Soft fruit	1–2 days

Vegetables

Green vegetables	3–4 days
Salad leaves	2–3 days

Dairy Food

Eggs	1 week
Milk	4–5 days
Yogurt	4–5 days

Non-dairy Alternatives

Soya milk	4–5 days
Silken tofu	3–4 days

Cook's Tip

Smoothies and fresh fruit and vegetable juices are best drunk as soon as possible after you have prepared them. If you do need to store a smoothie, keep it for no more than a few hours, well sealed in the refrigerator; add a few drops of lemon juice to help prevent discolouration.

1

Fruit and Vegetable Crushes

Apple Crush

Makes 300ml (¹/₂ pint)

175g (6oz) strawberries

150ml (¹/₄ pint) freshly pressed apple juice or 2 dessert apples, juiced

strawberry leaves or mint leaves to decorate

1 Remove the hulls from the strawberries, then wash and pat the fruit dry with kitchen paper. Put on a tray and freeze for about 40 minutes or until firm.

2 When ready to serve, put the frozen strawberries into a blender and pour in the juice. Blend until smooth and slushy. Pile into a serving glass and decorate.

Try Something Different

Use raspberries instead of strawberries.

EASY	NUTRITIONAL INFORMATION		Serves
Preparation Time 5 minutes, plus freezing	**Per Serving** 100 calories, 0.3g fat (of which 0g saturates), 23.9g carbohydrate, 0g salt	Vegetarian Gluten free • Dairy free	**1**

Cook's Tip

This is a fairly thick smoothie. You may prefer to thin it down with water or some freshly pressed orange juice.

Berry Orange

Makes 400ml (14fl oz)

2 medium oranges

50g (2oz) cranberries, thawed if frozen, juices reserved

50g (2oz) raspberries, thawed if frozen, juices reserved

1 tsp clear honey (optional)

1 Using a zester or a small, sharp knife, remove some strips of orange peel for decoration, if you like, then cut off the remainder, removing as much of the white pith as possible. Chop the flesh roughly, discarding any pips.

2 If using fresh cranberries and raspberries, remove the stalks and hulls as necessary, then wash and pat the fruit dry with kitchen paper. Put into a blender and, if the fruit has been frozen, add the juices.

3 Add the orange and blend until smooth. Taste and sweeten if necessary. Pour into two serving glasses and decorate with the orange peel to serve.

Serves 2	EASY	NUTRITIONAL INFORMATION	
	Preparation Time 10 minutes	**Per Serving** 71 calories, 0.3g fat (of which 0.1g saturates), 16.2g carbohydrate, 0g salt	Vegetarian Gluten free • Dairy free

Cook's Tip

If you prefer a thinner smoothie, add a little water.

Taste of the Tropics

Makes 300ml (¹/₂ pint)

700g (1¹/₂lb) pineapple

275g (10oz) mango

1 kiwi fruit

150ml (¹/₄ pint) tropical fruit juice

1 Peel and core the pineapple and chop the flesh roughly. Slice the flesh off the central stone of the mango, then peel and chop.

2 Cut two thin slices of kiwi fruit and set aside. Peel the remainder and put into a blender with the pineapple, mango and tropical fruit juice.

3 Blend until smooth and thick, then pour into two glasses. Decorate with the reserved kiwi fruit.

EASY	NUTRITIONAL INFORMATION	Serves
Preparation Time 10 minutes	**Per Serving** 262 calories, 1.2g fat (of which 0.2g saturates), 64.2g carbohydrate, 0g salt Vegetarian Gluten free • Dairy free	**2**

Passionate Papaya

Makes 150ml (¹/₄ pint)

¹/₂ medium papaya

¹/₂ lime

2 passion fruit

1 Peel the papaya and scoop out the black seeds. Put a few slices aside for decoration.

2 Roughly chop the flesh and put into a blender. Remove a thin strip of lime zest and set aside.

3 Squeeze the lime juice into the blender. Halve the passion fruit and scoop the seeds and pulp into the blender. Blend until smooth, pour into a glass and decorate with the reserved lime zest and papaya slices.

Serves 1	EASY	NUTRITIONAL INFORMATION	
	Preparation Time 10 minutes	**Per Serving** 83 calories, 0.3g fat (of which 0g saturates), 19.3g carbohydrate, 0g salt	Vegetarian Gluten free • Dairy free

Blue Orange

Makes 300ml (¹/₂ pint)

175g (6oz) blueberries, thawed if frozen, juices reserved

2 medium oranges

1–2 tsp maple syrup (optional)

a few ice cubes

1 If using fresh blueberries, wash and pat dry with kitchen paper. Put the berries into a blender. If the fruit has been frozen, add the juices as well.

2 Using a sharp knife, peel the oranges, removing as much of the white pith as possible. Chop the flesh roughly, discarding any pips, and put into the blender.

3 Blend for a few seconds until smooth. Taste and add maple syrup, if you like. Put ice in a large glass and pour in the smoothie.

EASY	NUTRITIONAL INFORMATION		Serves
Preparation Time 10 minutes	**Per Serving** 211 calories, 0.3g fat (of which 0g saturates), 50g carbohydrate, 0g salt	Vegetarian Gluten-free • Dairy free	**1**

Queen Peach

Makes 300ml (½ pint)

2 ripe peaches

250g (9oz) pineapple

1 small, ripe banana

1 Wash the peaches and pat dry with kitchen paper, then cut them in half. Remove the stones and roughly chop the flesh.

2 Peel and core the pineapple and chop roughly. Peel the banana and chop roughly.

3 Put all the fruit into a blender and whizz until thick and smooth. Pour into a glass.

Serves 1	EASY	NUTRITIONAL INFORMATION	
	Preparation Time 10 minutes	**Per Serving** 228 calories, 0.9g fat (of which 0.1g saturates), 55.2g carbohydrate, 0g salt	Vegetarian Gluten free • Dairy free

Cool Green Melon

Makes 600ml (1 pint)

500g (1lb 2oz) green-fleshed melon, such as Galia

250g (9oz) honeydew melon

150ml (¼ pint) freshly pressed apple juice or 2 dessert apples, juiced

4 fresh mint sprigs

a few ice cubes

2 strawberries, sliced, to decorate

1 Cut the melons into slices and slice off the skin. Discard the seeds and chop the flesh roughly. Put into a blender.

2 Pour in the apple juice. Wash and shake dry the mint and add to the blender.

3 Blend for a few seconds until smooth. Pour it over ice cubes and decorate with strawberries to serve.

Serves 2	EASY	NUTRITIONAL INFORMATION	
	Preparation Time 10 minutes	**Per Serving** 120 calories, 0g fat (of which 0g saturates), 30g carbohydrate, 0.0g salt [to come]	Vegetarian Gluten free • Dairy free

Try Something Different

For a less intense flavour, blend 125g (4oz) blackcurrants with 50g (2oz) strawberries.

Makes 400ml (14fl oz)

175g (6oz) blackcurrants, thawed if frozen, juices reserved

150ml (¼ pint) freshly pressed apple juice or 2 dessert apples, juiced

5 fresh mint sprigs

1–2 tsp clear honey (optional)

a few ice cubes

Black Beauty

1 If using fresh blackcurrants, wash and pat them dry with kitchen paper and pull off the stalks. Put the blackcurrants into a blender. If they have been frozen, add the juices as well.

2 Pour in the apple juice. Wash and shake dry the mint and add three sprigs to the blender.

3 Blend for a few seconds until smooth. Taste and add honey if necessary. Pour it over ice cubes and decorate with the remaining mint to serve.

EASY	NUTRITIONAL INFORMATION		Serves
Preparation Time 10 minutes	**Per Serving** 51 calories, 0.1g fat (of which 0g saturates), 12.5g carbohydrate, 0g salt	Vegetarian Gluten free • Dairy free	**2**

Gingery Watermelon

Makes 300ml (¹/₂ pint)
250g (9oz) watermelon
125g (4oz) red seedless grapes
1cm (¹/₂ in) piece fresh root ginger
a few ice cubes

1 Slice off a thin piece of watermelon for decoration and set aside. Peel, remove the seeds and roughly chop the flesh. Put into a blender.

2 Wash and pat the grapes dry with kitchen paper, and add to the blender.

3 Peel the ginger and chop roughly. Add to the blender and whizz for a few seconds until smooth. Pour over ice in a large glass and decorate with the reserved watermelon to serve.

Try Something Different

Red grapes are very sweet. If they are unavailable, choose seedless green grapes, or black ones – you will need to remove the seeds.

EASY	NUTRITIONAL INFORMATION		Serves
Preparation Time 5 minutes	**Per Serving** 153 calories, 0.9g fat (of which 0.3g saturates), 37g carbohydrate, 0g salt	Vegetarian Gluten free • Dairy free	**1**

Try Something Different

Wild rocket can be used instead of the watercress.

Cucumber and Carrot Combo

Makes 400ml (14fl oz)

375g (13oz) cucumber

25g (1oz) watercress

150ml (¼ pint) freshly pressed carrot juice or 3 medium carrots, 250g (9oz), juiced

freshly ground black pepper

a few ice cubes

1 Wash and pat the cucumber dry with kitchen paper. Slice lengthways and set aside a slice for decoration. Discard the seeds from the remaining cucumber, then chop the flesh roughly.

2 Put into a blender. Wash and shake dry the watercress, trim if necessary, and put all but two sprigs in the blender.

3 Pour in the carrot juice and season lightly with black pepper. Blend until smooth. Pour over ice and sprinkle with extra pepper, if you like. Decorate with cucumber and a sprig of watercress.

Serves 2	EASY	NUTRITIONAL INFORMATION	
	Preparation Time 5 minutes	**Per Serving** 66 calories, 0.7g fat (of which 0.2g saturates), 12.9g carbohydrate, 0.1g salt	Vegetarian Gluten free • Dairy free

Fruity Carrot with Ginger

Makes 400ml (14fl oz)

2 medium oranges

1cm (½ in) piece fresh root ginger

150ml (¼ pint) freshly pressed apple juice or 2 dessert apples, juiced

150ml (¼ pint) freshly pressed carrot juice or 3 medium carrots, 250g (9oz), juiced

mint leaves to decorate

1 Using a sharp knife, cut a slice of orange and set aside for decoration. Cut off the peel from the oranges, removing as much of the white pith as possible. Chop the flesh roughly, discarding any pips, and put into a blender.

2 Peel and roughly chop the ginger, and add to the blender.

3 Pour in the apple and carrot juice, and blend until smooth. Divide between two glasses, decorate with quartered orange slices and a mint leaf and serve.

EASY	NUTRITIONAL INFORMATION		Serves
Preparation Time 10 minutes	**Per Serving** 128 calories, 0.6g fat (of which 0.2g saturates), 30.1g carbohydrate, 0.1g salt	Vegetarian Gluten free • Dairy free	**2**

Pink Mango

Makes 300ml (¹/₂ pint)

¹/₂ pink grapefruit

300g (11oz) mango

150ml (¹/₄ pint) freshly pressed apple juice
or 2 dessert apples, juiced

apple slices to decorate (optional)

1 Using a sharp knife, cut off the peel from the grapefruit, removing as much of the white pith as possible. Chop roughly, discarding any pips, and put into a blender.

2 Slice the flesh off the central stone of the mango, and reserve two small slices for decoration, if you like, then peel the remainder, chop and put into the blender.

3 Pour in the apple juice and blend for a few seconds until smooth. Divide between two glasses, decorate with mango and apple slices, if using.

Try Something Different

Use an orange instead of the pink grapefruit.

Serves 2	EASY		NUTRITIONAL INFORMATION	
	Preparation Time 5 minutes		**Per Serving** 126 calories, 0.4g fat (of which 0.2g saturates), 31.3g carbohydrate, 0g salt	Vegetarian Gluten free • Dairy free

Try Something Different

For a spicier smoothie, add a dash of Tabasco along with the lime juice.

Avocado and Pear

Makes 250ml (9fl oz)

1 small lemon

2 ripe dessert pears

1 small, ripe avocado

juice of 1 lime

1 Peel the lemon, removing as much of the white pith as possible. Chop the flesh and remove any pips. Put into a blender.

2 Peel, core and chop the pears, then put into the blender. Halve the avocado, remove the stone and peel. Chop roughly and put into the blender with the lime juice.

3 Blend until smooth, then pour into a glass to serve.

Serves 1	EASY	NUTRITIONAL INFORMATION	
	Preparation Time 5 minutes	**Per Serving** 310 calories, 19.6g fat (of which 4.1g saturates), 31.9g carbohydrate, 0g salt	Vegetarian Gluten free • Dairy free

Cook's Tip

Wheatgrass deteriorates quickly, so it should be juiced once everything else has been prepared to ensure that you are getting the freshest drink possible. You can buy wheatgrass from a health-food shop; it is sold sprouting, in cartons like mustard and cress. Snip the wheatgrass as close to the base as possible using scissors, and measure it tightly bunched in 'rounds' like spaghetti – a 5cm (2in) round will yield about 50ml (2fl oz) juice.

Wheatgrass Salad

Makes 200ml (7fl oz)

25g (1oz) fresh parsley

25g (1oz) fresh coriander

75g (3oz) watercress

75g (3oz) cucumber

5cm (2in) round wheatgrass (see Cook's Tip)

water, well chilled (optional)

1 Wash and shake dry the herbs and watercress, and put into a blender.

2 Wash and pat the cucumber dry with kitchen paper. Peel if you like, then roughly chop and put into the blender.

3 Wash and shake the wheatgrass dry, then juice in a slow-turning or wheatgrass juicer. Add the juice to the cucumber and herbs. Blend for a few seconds until well blended, then serve immediately, topped up with chilled water, if you like.

EASY	NUTRITIONAL INFORMATION		Serves
Preparation Time 10 minutes	**Per Serving** 43 calories, 1.5g fat (of which 0.2g saturates), 2.9g carbohydrate, 0.1g salt	Vegetarian Gluten free • Dairy free	1

2

Creamy Combinations

Apricot and Orange

Makes about 450ml (³/₄ pint)

400g (14oz) canned apricots in natural juice

150g (5oz) apricot yogurt

200–250ml (7–9fl oz) unsweetened orange juice

1 Put the apricots, yogurt and orange juice into a blender or food processor and whizz for 1 minute or until smooth.

2 Chill well, then pour into two glasses and serve.

Serves 2	EASY	NUTRITIONAL INFORMATION	
	Preparation Time 5 minutes, plus chilling	**Per Serving** 172 calories, 0.8g fat (of which 0.3g saturates), 39.1g carbohydrate, 0.2g salt	Vegetarian • Gluten free

Strawberry and Pineapple Smoothie

Makes 450ml (³/₄ pint)

225g (8oz) strawberries

200–250ml (7–9fl oz) unsweetened pineapple juice

150g (5oz) low-fat strawberry yogurt

1 Remove the hulls from the strawberries, then wash and pat the fruit dry with kitchen paper. Set aside one or two strawberries for decoration, then put all the ingredients into a blender and whiz for 1 minute or until smooth.

2 Chill well, then pour into two glasses, decorate with halved strawberries and serve.

EASY	NUTRITIONAL INFORMATION		Serves
Preparation Time 5 minutes, plus chilling	**Per Serving** 145 calories, 0.7g fat (of which 0.3g saturates), 32.4g carbohydrate, 0.1g salt	Vegetarian • Gluten free	**2**

Summer Berry Smoothie

Makes 900ml (1¹/₂ pints)

2 large, ripe bananas, about 450g (1lb)

150g (5oz) natural yogurt

500g (1lb 2oz) fresh or frozen summer berries

1 Peel and chop the bananas, then put into a blender. Add the yogurt and 150ml (¹/₄ pint) water, then whizz until smooth. Add the berries and whizz to a purée.

2 Sieve the mixture into a large jug, using the back of a ladle to press it through the sieve. Pour into six glasses and serve.

Try Something Different

Six ripe apricots or 16 ready-to-eat dried apricots or 400g (14oz) canned apricots in natural juice can be used instead of the berries.

EASY	NUTRITIONAL INFORMATION		Serves
Preparation Time 10 minutes	**Per Serving** 108 calories, 0.6g fat (of which 0.2g trace saturates), 24.3g carbohydrate, 0.1g salt	Vegetarian • Gluten free	**6**

Prune, Apple and Cinnamon Smoothie

Makes about 450ml ($^3/_4$ pint)

125g (4oz) ready-to-eat prunes

$^1/_4$ tsp ground cinnamon

300–350ml (10–12fl oz) unsweetened apple juice

4 tbsp Greek yogurt, plus 1 tbsp to decorate

1 Set aside two prunes for decoration. Using scissors, snip the remaining prunes finely into a bowl and sprinkle with cinnamon, then pour in the apple juice. Cover the bowl and leave to stand overnight.

2 Put the prune mixture into a blender or food processor, add the yogurt and whizz for 1 minute or until smooth. Chill well, then pour into two glasses and decorate with a swirl of yogurt and a halved prune to serve.

Serves 2	EASY		NUTRITIONAL INFORMATION	
	Preparation Time 10 minutes, plus overnight soaking and chilling		**Per Serving** 180 calories, 3.5g fat (of which 1.6g saturates), 36.7g carbohydrate, 0.1g salt	Vegetarian • Gluten free

Blue Cherry

Makes 450ml (³/₄ pint)

125g (4oz) fresh cherries

125g (4oz) blueberries, thawed if frozen, juices reserved

125g (4oz) low-fat natural dairy or soya yogurt, well chilled

125ml (4fl oz) low-fat dairy or non-dairy milk, well chilled

1–2 tsp maple syrup, to taste

1 Wash and pat the cherries dry with kitchen paper. Remove the stones and put the cherries into a blender. Wash and pat dry the blueberries if using fresh.

2 Add the blueberries to the blender. If the fruit has been frozen, add the juices as well. Spoon in the yogurt and pour in the milk.

3 Blend until thick and smooth. Sweeten to taste with maple syrup, then pour into two glasses to serve.

EASY	NUTRITIONAL INFORMATION		Serves
Preparation Time 10 minutes	**Per Serving** 122 calories, 0.9g fat (of which 0.4g saturates), 23.8g carbohydrate, 0.2g salt	Vegetarian • Gluten free	**2**

Spiced Plum Cooler

Makes 600ml (1 pint)

2 cardamom pods

4 medium plums

a pinch of ground cinnamon, plus extra to dust

125g (4oz) low-fat vanilla-flavoured yogurt, well chilled

1 tsp thick honey

125ml (4fl oz) low-fat milk, well chilled

cinnamon sticks to decorate

1 Peel the green casing from the cardamom pods and remove the black seeds. Crush the seeds finely using a mortar and pestle.

2 Wash and pat the plums dry with kitchen paper, then cut them in half and remove the stones. Put into a blender with the crushed cardamom and a pinch of cinnamon.

3 Spoon in the yogurt and honey, and pour in the milk. Blend until creamy and smooth. Pour into two large glasses. Dust with extra cinnamon and decorate with a cinnamon stick.

Serves 2	EASY		NUTRITIONAL INFORMATION	
	Preparation Time 10 minutes		**Per Serving** 105 calories, 0.8g fat (of which 0.4g saturates), 21.2g carbohydrate, 0.2g salt	Vegetarian • Gluten free

Try Something Different

For extra flavour choose fruit-flavoured soya yogurt.
Use calcium-enriched soya milk for extra nutrients.
Six ready-to-eat dried apricots can be used instead of
fresh.

Peachy Soya Blend

Makes 600ml (1 pint)

1 ripe peach

2 ripe apricots

$\frac{1}{2}$ small orange

125g (4oz) peach-flavoured soya yogurt

125ml (4fl oz) unsweetened soya milk, well chilled

1 Wash the peach and apricots and pat dry with kitchen paper. Halve and remove the stones, then chop the fruit roughly and put into a blender.

2 Peel the orange, removing as much of the white pith as possible. Chop the orange flesh and remove any seeds. Put into the blender. Spoon in the yogurt and pour in the milk.

3 Blend for a few seconds until smooth, then pour into two tall glasses.

EASY	NUTRITIONAL INFORMATION		Serves
Preparation Time minutes, plus chilling	**Per Serving** 112 calories, 2.3g fat (of which 0.4g saturates), 19.2g carbohydrate, 0.1g salt	Vegetarian Gluten free • Dairy free	**2**

Summer in a Glass

Makes 600ml (1 pint)

½ pink grapefruit

½ melon

1 small, ripe banana

225g (8oz) low-fat natural dairy or soya yogurt

1–2 tsp thick honey

a few ice cubes

mint sprigs to decorate

1 Using a sharp knife, cut off the peel from the grapefruit, taking off as much of the white pith as possible. Cut into segments, then chop the flesh roughly, discarding any pips, and put into a blender.

2 Remove the melon seeds and skin. Chop the flesh roughly and add to the blender.

3 Peel the banana, chop roughly and add to the blender. Add the yogurt, and honey to taste. Blend for a few seconds until smooth. Pour over ice in two glasses and decorate.

Serves 2	EASY	NUTRITIONAL INFORMATION	
	Preparation Time 10 minutes	**Per Serving** 176 calories, 1.5g fat (of which 0.6g saturates), 35.5g carbohydrate, 0.4g salt	Vegetarian • Gluten free

Cook's Tip

Silken tofu is very smooth and is the best for blending in drinks. It is available fresh or vacuum-packed in cartons. Firmer types can be used but give a grainier texture when blended.

Creamy Dairy-free Banana

Makes 400ml (14fl oz)

1 large, ripe banana

125g (4oz) silken tofu, well chilled

175ml (6fl oz) unsweetened soya milk, well chilled

2 tsp thick honey

a few drops of vanilla extract

1 Peel the banana and slice thickly. Put into a blender.

2 Drain the tofu, mash lightly with a fork and add to the blender.

3 Pour in the milk and add the honey with a few drops of vanilla extract. Blend for a few seconds until thick and smooth. Pour into a large glass and serve.

Serves 1	EASY	NUTRITIONAL INFORMATION	
	Preparation Time 5 minutes	**Per Serving** 238 calories, 8.3g fat (of which 1.2g saturates), 24.7g carbohydrate, 0.2g salt	Vegetarian Gluten free • Dairy free

Virgin Mary Cooler

Makes 750ml (1¼ pints)

8 ripe medium vine tomatoes

a pinch of celery salt

a dash of Worcestershire sauce

a few drops of Tabasco sauce

150g (5oz) low-fat natural dairy or soya yogurt, well chilled

6 ice cubes, crushed

2 small celery sticks with leaves, to serve

1 Wash the tomatoes and pat dry with kitchen paper. Cut into quarters, then put into a blender.

2 Season the tomatoes with celery salt, Worcestershire sauce and Tabasco sauce.

3 Spoon in the yogurt and blend until smooth. Fill two large glasses with crushed ice, pour in the tomato drink and serve with the celery sticks.

EASY	NUTRITIONAL INFORMATION		Serves
Preparation Time 5 minutes	**Per Serving** 78 calories, 1.4g fat (of which 0.6g saturates), 12.2g carbohydrate, 0.3g salt	Gluten free • Dairy free	**2**

Raspberry and Kiwi Smoothie

Makes 500–600ml (18fl oz–1 pint)

3 kiwi fruit

200g (7oz) fresh or frozen raspberries, thawed if frozen, juices reserved

200–250ml (7–9fl oz) unsweetened orange juice

4 tbsp Greek yogurt

1 Peel and roughly chop the kiwi fruit and put into a blender. If using fresh raspberries, remove the hulls, then wash and pat the fruit dry with kitchen paper. Add to the blender. If the fruit has been frozen, add the juices as well.

2 Pour in the orange juice and yogurt. Blend until smooth, then serve.

Serves 2	EASY		NUTRITIONAL INFORMATION	
	Preparation Time 8 minutes		**Per Serving** 140 calories, 3.9g fat (of which 1.7g saturates), 23.6g carbohydrate, 0.1g salt	Vegetarian • Gluten free

Passion Fruit, Grape and Banana Smoothie

Makes 900ml (1¹/₂ pints)

4 ripe passion fruit

150g (5oz) low-fat natural yogurt, plus 1 tbsp to decorate

4 ripe bananas, about 550g (1¹/₄lb)

225g (8oz) seedless white grapes

8 ice cubes, crushed

1 Chill four tall glasses in the freezer. Cut the passion fruit in half and remove the pulp. Put 1 tbsp of pulp aside for decoration and put the remainder into a blender with the yogurt.

2 Peel the bananas and roughly chop them. Add to the blender with the grapes and whizz until smooth. (The edible passion fruit pips will remain whole.) Pour into the chilled glasses, stir in the ice, and decorate with the 1 tbsp yogurt mixed with the reserved passion fruit pulp, then serve.

EASY	NUTRITIONAL INFORMATION		Serves
Preparation Time 5 minutes, plus chilling	**Per Serving** 191 calories, 0.9g fat (of which 0.4g saturates), 44.3g carbohydrate, 0.1g salt	Vegetarian • Gluten free	**4**

Carrot with a Bite

Makes 300ml (½ pint)

1 medium orange

150ml (¼ pint) freshly pressed carrot juice or 3 medium carrots, 250g (9oz), juiced

150g (5oz) low-fat natural dairy or soya yogurt, well chilled

a few drops of Tabasco sauce

1 Peel the orange, removing as much of the white pith as possible. Chop the flesh and remove any pips, then put into a blender.

2 Pour in the carrot juice. Add the yogurt and a few drops of Tabasco sauce. Blend until smooth and pour into a glass.

Serves 1	EASY	NUTRITIONAL INFORMATION	
	Preparation Time 10 minutes	Per Serving 216 calories, 2.4g fat (of which 1g saturates), 41.2g carbohydrate, 0.5g salt	Vegetarian • Gluten free

Try Something Different

Instead of mango, use 2 nectarines or peaches, or 175g (6oz) soft seasonal fruits such as raspberries, strawberries or blueberries.

Mango and Oat Smoothie

Makes 600ml (1 pint)

150g (5oz) natural yogurt

1 small mango

2 tbsp oats

4 ice cubes, crushed

1 Put the yogurt into a blender. Slice the flesh off the central stone of the mango, then peel and chop. Set aside a little chopped mango to decorate, then add the remainder to the blender.

2 Add the oats to the blender and whizz until smooth. Divide the ice between two glasses, pour in the mango drink and serve immediately, decorated with chopped mango.

Serves 2	EASY	NUTRITIONAL INFORMATION	
	Preparation Time 5 minutes	**Per Serving** 145 calories, 2.2g fat (of which 0.5g saturates), 27.1g carbohydrate, 0.2g salt	Vegetarian • Gluten free

Cook's Tip

If you're on a dairy-free diet or need an alternative to milk-based products, swap the yogurt for soya yogurt.

Cranberry and Mango Smoothie

Makes 600ml (1 pint)

1 ripe mango, stone removed

250ml (9fl oz) cranberry juice

150g (5oz) natural yogurt

1 Peel and roughly chop the mango and put into a blender with the cranberry juice. Blend for 1 minute.

2 Add the yogurt and blend until smooth, then pour into two glasses.

EASY	NUTRITIONAL INFORMATION		Serves
Preparation Time 5 minutes	**Per Serving** 133 calories, 1g fat (of which 0.5g saturates), 28.6g carbohydrate, 0.2g salt	Vegetarian • Gluten free	**2**

3

Vitality Drinks

Morning-after Detoxer

Papaya Booster

Strawberry and Camomile Calmer

Green Tea Pick-me-up

Raspberry Rascal Booster

Busy Bee's Comforter

Mega-Vitamin C Tonic

Dairy-free Nutty Milk

Berry Uplifter

Flaxen Pear

Creamy Oat and Raspberry Cooler

Tofu and Avocado Charger

Banana Vitality Shake

Brazil Nut and Banana Smoothie

Morning-after Detoxer

Makes 600ml (1 pint)

200g (7oz) cooked, peeled baby beetroot in natural juice

15g (½ oz) fresh root ginger

juice of 1 lemon

150ml (¼ pint) freshly pressed carrot juice
or 2 medium carrots, 250g (9oz), juiced

150ml (¼ pint) freshly pressed apple juice
or 2 dessert apples, juiced

1 Roughly chop the beetroot and put into a blender with the juices from the pack.

2 Peel and roughly chop the ginger and add to the blender.

3 Pour in the carrot and apple juices and blend until smooth. Pour into two glasses and serve immediately.

Cook's Tip

If you find the smoothie too concentrated, thin it with a little chilled water.

Try Something Different

For a more powerful detoxer, juice 225g (8oz) raw beetroot and 5cm (2in) piece fresh root ginger, peeled, and mix with the other juices.

EASY	NUTRITIONAL INFORMATION		Serves
Preparation Time 10 minutes	**Per Serving** 115 calories, 0.6g fat (of which 0.2g saturates), 26.4g carbohydrate, 0.2g salt	Vegetarian Gluten free • Dairy free	**2**

Papaya Booster

Makes 600ml (1 pint)

1 small papaya

1 ripe peach

2 passion fruit

200ml (7fl oz) freshly squeezed orange juice
or 2 large oranges, juiced

1–2 acidophilus capsules (optional)

1 Peel the papaya, cut in half and scoop out and discard the seeds. Put the flesh into a blender. Wash the peach and pat dry with kitchen paper, then halve, remove the stone and put into the blender.

2 Halve the passion fruit and scoop out the seeds and pulp into a small sieve. Strain the juice into the blender. Pour in the orange juice and blend for a few seconds until smooth.

3 Open up the acidophilus capsules, if using, and stir into the smoothie. Pour into two large glasses and serve immediately.

Serves 2	EASY	NUTRITIONAL INFORMATION	
	Preparation Time 10 minutes	**Per Serving** 107 calories, 0.4g fat (of which 0g saturates), 25.6g carbohydrate, 0.1g salt	Vegetarian Gluten free • Dairy free

Try Something Different

Camomile tea bags are very convenient and easy to use, but freshly dried flowers will give a stronger flavour.

Strawberry and Camomile Calmer

Makes 600ml (1 pint)

2 camomile tea bags

5cm (2in) piece cinnamon stick

150ml (¼ pint) boiling water

175g (6oz) strawberries

150ml (¼ pint) freshly pressed apple juice or 2 large dessert apples, juiced

1 Put the tea bags and cinnamon stick into a small, heatproof jug and pour in 150ml (¼ pint) boiling water. Leave to infuse for 5 minutes, then discard the bags and cinnamon stick. Leave to cool.

2 When ready to serve, remove the hulls from the strawberries, then wash and pat the fruit dry with kitchen paper. Put into a blender.

3 Pour in the apple juice and cold camomile tea. Blend for a few seconds until smooth. Pour into two tall glasses and serve.

EASY

Preparation Time
5 minutes, plus infusing and cooling

NUTRITIONAL INFORMATION

Per Serving
52 calories, 0.2g fat (of which 0g saturates), 12.7g carbohydrate, 0g salt

Vegetarian
Gluten free • Dairy free

Serves
2

Try Something Different

For extra zing, add a 5cm (2in) piece fresh root ginger, peeled and chopped, to the blender in step 2.

Green Tea Pick-me-up

Makes 300ml (½ pint)

1 tsp, or 1 teabag, good-quality Japanese green tea

1 ripe kiwi fruit

8 fresh lychees

a few ice cubes

1 Put the tea or teabag in a heatproof jug and pour in 200ml (7fl oz) boiling water. Leave to infuse for 3 minutes, then strain to remove the tea leaves or discard the teabag. Leave to cool.

2 When ready to serve, peel and roughly chop the kiwi fruit. Put into a blender. Peel the lychees, then cut in half and remove the stones.

3 Add to the blender with the cold tea. Blend until smooth and pour over ice in a glass to serve.

Serves 1	EASY	NUTRITIONAL INFORMATION	
	Preparation Time 10 minutes, plus infusing and cooling	**Per Serving** 99 calories, 0.4g fat (of which 0g saturates), 23.5g carbohydrate, 0g salt	Vegetarian Gluten free • Dairy free

Cook's Tip

If you find this smoothie too thick, water it down a little.

Raspberry Rascal Booster

Makes 300ml (¹/₂ pint)

225g (8oz) raspberries, thawed if frozen, juices reserved

1 medium orange

2 tsp thick honey

1 If using fresh raspberries, remove the hulls, then wash and pat the fruit dry with kitchen paper. Set two raspberries to one side for decoration, and put the rest into a blender. If the fruit has been frozen, add the juices as well.

2 Peel the orange, removing as much of the white pith as possible. Chop the flesh roughly, discarding any pips, and put into blender. Add the honey. Blend until smooth, pour into a glass, decorate with the raspberries and serve immediately.

EASY	NUTRITIONAL INFORMATION		Serves
Preparation Time 5 minutes	**Per Serving** 147 calories, 0.8g fat (of which 0.2g saturates), 32.8g carbohydrate, 0g salt	Vegetarian Gluten free • Dairy free	**1**

Busy Bee's Comforter

Makes 200ml (7fl oz)

2 lemons

150ml (¼ pint) full-fat natural or soya yogurt, at room temperature

1–2 tsp thick honey

2–3 tsp bee pollen grains or equivalent in capsule form (see Health Tip)

1 Using a sharp knife, cut off the peel from one lemon, removing as much of the white pith as possible. Chop the flesh roughly, discarding any pips, and put into a blender. Squeeze the juice from the remaining lemon and add to the blender.

2 Spoon in the yogurt and blend until smooth. Taste and sweeten with honey as necessary. Stir in the bee pollen, then pour into a glass and serve.

Health Tip

Not suitable for those with an allergy to pollen, such as hayfever sufferers.

Try Something Different

Use oranges instead of lemons.

Serves 1	EASY	NUTRITIONAL INFORMATION	
	Preparation Time 5 minutes	**Per Serving** 130 calories, 1.5g fat (of which 0.8g saturates), 23.5g carbohydrate, 0.3g salt	Vegetarian • Gluten free

Try Something Different

For a refreshing, longer and less concentrated drink, divide this smoothie between two glasses and top up with sparkling mineral water.

Mega-Vitamin C Tonic

Makes 200ml (7fl oz)

1 large orange

1 lemon

1 lime

½ pink grapefruit

1–2 tsp clear honey

crushed ice

slices of citrus fruit to decorate

1 Using a sharp knife, cut off the peel from all the citrus fruit, removing as much of the white pith as possible. Chop the flesh roughly, discarding any pips, and put into a blender.

2 Add the honey to taste and blend for a few seconds until smooth.

3 Pour over crushed ice in a glass and decorate with citrus fruit to serve.

Serves 1	EASY	NUTRITIONAL INFORMATION	
	Preparation Time 10 minutes	**Per Serving** 144 calories, 0.3g fat (of which 0g saturates), 34.7g carbohydrate, 0g salt	Vegetarian Gluten free • Dairy free

Cook's Tips

This 'milk' is an excellent source of protein and is excellent served over ice.
Store opened packs of nuts and seeds, well sealed, in the refrigerator to keep them as fresh as possible.

Makes 350ml (12fl oz)

25g (1oz) whole blanched almonds

25g (1oz) shelled pecan nut halves

1 tbsp pumpkin seeds

300ml (½ pint) unsweetened soya milk

½ tsp ground cinnamon, plus extra to dust

1 tsp clear honey

a few ice cubes (optional)

Dairy-free Nutty Milk

1 Grind the nuts and seeds together in a spice grinder or food processor. The mixture needs to be very fine to obtain a good blend.

2 Transfer to a small jug and gradually blend in the soya milk. Mix in the cinnamon and honey.

3 Pour into a glass, over ice if you like, and dust with extra cinnamon.

EASY	NUTRITIONAL INFORMATION		Serves
Preparation Time 5 minutes	**Per Serving** 512 calories, 39.8g fat (of which 3.9g saturates), 14.8g carbohydrate, 0.3g salt	Vegetarian Gluten free • Dairy free	**1**

Berry Uplifter

Makes 400ml (14fl oz)

175g (6oz) blueberries, thawed if frozen, juices reserved

50g (2oz) cranberries, thawed if frozen, juices reserved

200ml (7fl oz) freshly pressed orange juice or 2 medium oranges, juiced

1 tbsp wheatgerm

1–2 tsp thick honey

1 If using fresh berries, wash and pat them dry with kitchen paper and put into a blender. If the fruit has been frozen, add the juices as well.

2 Pour in the orange juice and add 2 tsp wheatgerm. Blend until smooth.

3 Taste and add honey to sweeten. Pour into a glass and serve sprinkled with the remaining wheatgerm.

Health Tip

Blueberries contain a substance that helps the gut to stay clean and healthy, and, like cranberries, they are rich in antioxidants.

Try Something Different

Use blackberries instead of blueberries: they are an excellent source of vitamin C.

EASY	NUTRITIONAL INFORMATION		Serves
Preparation Time 5 minutes	**Per Serving** 277 calories, 1.6g fat (of which 0.2g saturates), 61.9g carbohydrate, 0.1g salt	Vegetarian • Gluten free	**1**

Try Something Different

Replace the whole flaxseeds with 1 tbsp flaxseed oil, available from health food shops.

Makes 600ml (1 pint)

1 tbsp flaxseed (linseed)

2 ripe pears

150ml (¼ pint) low-fat dairy or soya milk, well chilled

150ml (¼ pint) low-fat natural or soya yogurt, well chilled

2 tsp clear honey (optional)

Flaxen Pear

1 Grind the seeds in a spice grinder or a pestle and mortar – the mixture needs to be very fine in order to obtain a good blend – and put in a blender.

2 Peel, core and chop the pears, then add to the blender.

3 Pour in the milk and add the yogurt. Blend until smooth and add honey to taste. Pour into two glasses and serve immediately.

Serves 2	EASY		NUTRITIONAL INFORMATION	
	Preparation Time 5 minutes		**Per Serving** 171 calories, 4.7g fat (of which 0.8g saturates), 25.8g carbohydrate, 0.3g salt	Vegetarian • Gluten free

Try Something Different

Use blackberries or strawberries instead of raspberries.

Creamy Oat and Raspberry Cooler

Makes 400ml (14fl oz)

175g (6oz) raspberries, thawed if frozen, juices reserved

100ml (3¹/₂fl oz) freshly squeezed orange juice or 1 large orange, juiced

100ml (3¹/₂fl oz) oat milk, well chilled

100ml (3¹/₂fl oz) low-fat natural or soya yogurt, well chilled

40g (1¹/₂oz) fine oatmeal

2 tsp wheat bran

2 tsp clear honey (optional)

1 If using fresh raspberries, remove the hulls, then wash and pat the fruit dry with kitchen paper. Put into a blender. If the fruit has been frozen, add the juices as well.

2 Pour in the orange juice and oat milk, and spoon in the yogurt. Add the oatmeal and 1 tsp wheat bran. Blend until smooth.

3 Taste and sweeten with honey if necessary. Pour into two glasses, sprinkle with the remaining wheat bran and serve.

EASY	NUTRITIONAL INFORMATION		Serves
Preparation Time 5 minutes	**Per Serving** 182 calories, 3.8g fat (of which 0.6g saturates), 29.4g carbohydrate, 0.2g salt	Vegetarian	**2**

Tofu and Avocado Charger

Makes 300ml (½ pint)

1 spring onion

1 small garlic clove

1 small, ripe avocado

25g (1oz) alfalfa sprouts, plus extra to garnish

125g (4oz) silken tofu

1 Trim and chop the spring onion, then peel and crush the garlic. Put both into a blender.

2 Halve the avocado and remove the stone. Peel and roughly chop the flesh, then add to the blender with the alfalfa sprouts.

3 Add the tofu and 125ml (4fl oz) well-chilled water, and blend until thick, creamy and smooth. Stir in more water until you get the texture you require, then pour into a glass and serve garnished with alfalfa.

Try Something Different

Add 25g (1oz) parsley, washed and shaken dry, for an even more nutritious smoothie.

Cook's Tip

For a thinner consistency, divide the smoothie between two glasses and top up with chilled water.

Serves 1	EASY	NUTRITIONAL INFORMATION	
	Preparation Time 5 minutes	**Per Serving** 291 calories, 24.7g fat (of which 4.8g saturates), 4.1g carbohydrate, 0g salt	Vegetarian Gluten free • Dairy free

Banana Vitality Shake

Makes 600ml (1 pint)

25g (1oz) whole shelled almonds

1 large, ripe banana

150ml (¼ pint) low-fat milk

150ml (¼ pint) low-fat natural yogurt

8g sachet powdered egg-white

2 tsp wheatgerm

1–2 tsp maple syrup

a pinch of freshly grated nutmeg

1 Grind the almonds in a spice grinder or food processor – the mixture needs to be very fine to obtain a good blend.

2 Peel and roughly chop the banana, then put into a blender with the ground almonds. Add the milk, yogurt, powdered eggwhite and wheatgerm to the blender and whizz for a few seconds until smooth.

3 Add maple syrup to taste, then pour into two glasses and serve immediately, sprinkled with nutmeg.

Serves 2	EASY		NUTRITIONAL INFORMATION	
	Preparation Time 10 minutes		**Per Serving** 246 calories, 8.7g fat (of which 1.2g saturates), 31.9g carbohydrate, 0.4g salt	Vegetarian

Cook's Tip

This is a lusciously thick, protein-rich drink; add more milk if you like.

Brazil Nut and Banana Smoothie

Makes 600ml (1 pint)

6 shelled Brazil nuts

1 lemon

1 small, ripe banana

1 small, ripe avocado

1 tsp clear honey

400ml (14fl oz) low-fat dairy or soya milk, well chilled

2 tsp wheatgerm

1 Grind the nuts in a spice grinder or food processor – the mixture needs to be very fine to obtain a good blend.

2 Using a sharp knife, cut off the peel from the lemon, removing as much of the white pith as possible. Chop the flesh roughly, discarding any pips. Peel and roughly chop the banana. Halve the avocado and remove the stone. Peel and roughly chop.

3 Put the nuts, lemon, banana and avocado into a blender with the honey and milk. Blend until smooth. Pour into two glasses and sprinkle with the wheatgerm.

EASY	NUTRITIONAL INFORMATION		Serves
Preparation Time 10 minutes	**Per Serving** 310 calories, 19.4g fat (of which 4.4g saturates), 24.8g carbohydrate, 0.3g salt [to come]	Vegetarian	**2**

4

Sheer Indulgence

Tickled Pink

Makes 900ml (1½ pints)

500g (1lb 2oz) watermelon

125g (4oz) strawberries

2 scoops lemon sorbet

a few drops of rosewater

150g (5oz) crushed ice

300ml (½ pint) cream soda or pink lemonade,
well chilled, to taste

1 Remove the seeds from the watermelon, then peel and roughly chop the flesh. Put into a blender. Remove the hulls from the strawberries, then wash and pat the fruit dry with kitchen paper. Add to the blender.

2 Add the lemon sorbet and a few drops of rosewater. Blend for a few seconds until smooth.

3 Put a scoop of ice into each of two large glasses and pour in the watermelon and strawberry juice. Top up with soda or lemonade.

Serves 2	EASY	NUTRITIONAL INFORMATION	
	Preparation Time 10 minutes	**Per Serving** 176 calories, 1g fat (of which 0.3g saturates), 42.6g carbohydrate, 0.1g salt	Vegetarian Gluten free • Dairy free

Try Something Different

Add a large, ripe banana and 175g (6oz) strawberries for a fruity combo.

Chocolate Caramel Shaker

Makes 750ml (1¼ pints)

1 milk chocolate Flake bar

225ml (8fl oz) full-fat milk

4 scoops chocolate ice cream

150g (5oz) crushed ice

2 tbsp caramel syrup

2 tsp dark chocolate sauce

1 Put two glasses into the freezer to chill. Crumble the chocolate Flake bar into a blender, reserving a little for decoration.

2 Add the milk, ice cream, crushed ice and caramel syrup. Blend until thick, creamy and smooth.

3 Pour into the glasses. Sprinkle with the reserved chocolate flake bar and drizzle with chocolate sauce. Serve immediately.

EASY	NUTRITIONAL INFORMATION		Serves
Preparation Time 5 minutes	**Per Serving** 499 calories, 24.2g fat (of which 11.6g saturates), 64.4g carbohydrate, 0.5g salt	Vegetarian • Gluten free	**2**

Toffee Apple-tastic

Makes 600ml (1 pint)

1 dessert apple

150ml (¼ pint) freshly pressed apple juice or 2 large dessert apples, juiced

150ml (¼ pint) low-fat milk, chilled

1 tbsp low-fat milk powder

a few ice cubes

2 tbsp toffee or caramel syrup or sauce

25g (1oz) fudge, chopped

1 Peel, core and roughly chop the apple. Put into a blender with the apple juice.

2 Pour in the milk and add the milk powder. Blend until thick and smooth.

3 Pour into two glasses over ice, and drizzle with the syrup or sauce. Sprinkle with fudge pieces and serve immediately.

EASY	NUTRITIONAL INFORMATION		Serves
Preparation Time 5 minutes	**Per Serving** 234 calories, 7.8g fat (of which 1.2g saturates), 40.2g carbohydrate, 0.2g salt	Vegetarian • Gluten free	**2**

Raspberry Ripple

Makes 300ml (¹/₂ pint)

175g (6oz) raspberries, thawed if frozen, juices reserved

125ml (4fl oz) low-fat milk, chilled

125ml (4fl oz) full-fat natural yogurt, chilled

1 scoop raspberry-flavoured frozen yogurt

2 tsp raspberry syrup or sauce

1 If using fresh raspberries, remove the hulls, then wash and pat the fruit dry with kitchen paper. Put into a blender. If the fruit has been frozen, add the juices as well.

2 Pour in the milk and add the yogurt. Blend until thick and creamy.

3 Pour into a glass and top with a scoop of frozen yogurt. Drizzle with the syrup or sauce and serve immediately.

Serves 1	EASY	NUTRITIONAL INFORMATION	
	Preparation Time 5 minutes	**Per Serving** 289 calories, 7g fat (of which 4g saturates), 45.4g carbohydrate, 0.5g salt	Vegetarian • Gluten free

Try Something Different

For an icier version, freeze the banana pieces for about 30 minutes or until firm, then blend them as in step 2.

Buttery Banana Freeze

Makes 400ml (14fl oz)

1 large, ripe banana

125ml (4fl oz) low-fat milk

2 scoops butterscotch-flavoured ice cream

25g (1oz) butterscotch, crushed, or fudge, chopped

1 Peel and roughly chop the banana, then put it into a blender.

2 Pour in the milk. Add one scoop of ice cream. Blend until smooth and thick.

3 Pour into a glass and top with the remaining scoop of ice cream and a sprinkling of crushed butterscotch. Serve immediately.

EASY	NUTRITIONAL INFORMATION		Serves
Preparation Time 5 minutes	**Per Serving** 442 calories, 13.6g fat (of which 8.6g saturates), 74.6g carbohydrate, 0.4g salt	Vegetarian • Gluten free	**1**

Try Something Different

Mocha Treat: Omit the orange and replace the orange sorbet with coffee ice cream.

Indulgent Chocolate Orange Treat

Makes 400ml (14fl oz)

75ml (2½ fl oz) double or whipping cream

1 tbsp chocolate syrup

1 medium orange

2 scoops orange sorbet

250ml (9fl oz) low-fat chocolate milk, chilled

cocoa powder to dust

1 Spoon the cream into a bowl and whip until it just forms soft peaks. Carefully fold in the chocolate syrup. Cover and chill until required.

2 Using a sharp knife, cut off the peel from the orange, removing as much of the white pith as possible. Chop the flesh roughly, discarding any pips, and put into a blender.

3 When ready to serve, add the sorbet to the blender and pour in the milk. Blend until thick and smooth. Pour into a glass and top with the whipped cream. Serve immediately dusted with cocoa.

Serves 2	EASY		NUTRITIONAL INFORMATION	
	Preparation Time 10 minutes		**Per Serving** 352 calories, 20.2g fat (of which 10.7g saturates), 39g carbohydrate, 0.3g salt	Vegetarian • Gluten free

Try Something Different

For a speedier version, use canned rhubarb in syrup. You will need about 150g (5oz) and 50ml (2fl oz) of the syrup.

Rhubarb and Raspberry Custard

Makes 350ml (12fl oz)

150g (5oz) rhubarb

2 tsp light muscovado sugar

75g (3oz) raspberries, thawed if frozen, juices reserved

100ml (3½fl oz) ready-made vanilla-flavoured custard, chilled

100ml (3½fl oz) low-fat milk, chilled

1 Trim the rhubarb, then wash and pat dry with kitchen paper. Cut into 2.5cm (1in) pieces and put into a small pan with 50ml (2fl oz) water and the sugar. Bring to the boil, cover and simmer for 5 minutes or until tender. Leave to cool.

2 If using fresh raspberries, remove the hulls, then wash and pat the fruit dry with kitchen paper. Put into a blender. If the fruit has been frozen, add the juices as well. Blend for a few seconds until smooth.

3 Tip the rhubarb and its cooking juices into a clean blender and add the custard and milk. Blend until smooth.

4 Pour into a glass and swirl in the raspberry purée using a stirrer. Serve immediately.

EASY		NUTRITIONAL INFORMATION		Serves
Preparation Time 10 minutes	**Cooking Time** 5 minutes, plus cooling	**Per Serving** 200 calories, 2.5g fat (of which 0.2g saturates), 36.4g carbohydrate, 0.3g salt	Vegetarian • Gluten free	**1**

Chocolate Frappé

Makes 400ml (14fl oz)

50g (2oz) fresh coconut, plus extra to decorate

175ml (6fl oz) light coconut milk

4 tbsp chocolate syrup

2 scoops chocolate ice cream

200g (7oz) crushed ice

1 tbsp plain chocolate shavings

1 Roughly chop the coconut and put into a blender.

2 Pour in the coconut milk, then add the chocolate syrup, ice cream and crushed ice. Blend until smooth and creamy.

3 Pour into two glasses and serve immediately, decorated with coconut and chocolate shavings.

Serves 2	EASY	NUTRITIONAL INFORMATION	
	Preparation Time 5 minutes	Per Serving 348 calories, 18.7g fat (of which 4.7g saturates), 43.6g carbohydrate, 0.5g salt	Vegetarian • Gluten free

Blueberry New Yorker

Makes 300ml (¹/₂ pint)

125g (4oz) blueberries, thawed if frozen, juices reserved

50g (2oz) medium-fat cream cheese, chilled

1 tbsp maple syrup

a few drops of vanilla extract

125ml (4fl oz) low-fat milk, chilled

1 digestive biscuit or butter biscuit, crumbled (optional)

1 If using fresh blueberries, remove the hulls, then wash and pat the fruit dry with kitchen paper. Put into a blender. If the fruit has been frozen, add the juices as well.

2 Spoon in the cream cheese and maple syrup, then add the vanilla extract. Pour in the milk and blend until thick and smooth.

3 Pour into a glass and serve sprinkled with crumbled biscuit, if you like.

Serves 1	EASY	NUTRITIONAL INFORMATION	
	Preparation Time 5 minutes	**Per Serving** 247 calories, 7.6g fat (of which 4.7g saturates), 37.2g carbohydrate, 0.3g salt	Vegetarian

Cook's Tip

To crush biscuits easily, put them in a clean plastic bag, seal and crush with a rolling pin.

Peanut Butter and Bourbons

Makes 600ml (1 pint)

2 small, ripe bananas

2 tbsp smooth peanut butter

2 scoops non-fat vanilla frozen yogurt

200ml (7fl oz) low-fat milk, chilled

6 chocolate Bourbon biscuits, finely crushed

1 Peel and roughly chop the bananas, then put into a blender. Spoon in the peanut butter and frozen yogurt.

2 Pour in the milk and blend until thick and smooth. Fold in all but 1 tbsp crushed biscuits.

3 Divide between two glasses and sprinkle with the remaining crumbled biscuits. Serve immediately.

EASY	NUTRITIONAL INFORMATION		Serves
Preparation Time 5 minutes	**Per Serving** 630 calories, 28.7g fat (of which 15.4g saturates), 83.6g carbohydrate, 0.5g salt	Vegetarian	**2**

Cook's Tip

Coconut cream is a thick, concentrated form of coconut compound and is available in cartons. Replace with reduced-fat coconut milk for a healthier version, if you like.

Try Something Different

Add a dash of rum or two pieces of stem ginger in syrup.

Caribbean Dream

Makes 400ml (14fl oz)

200g (7oz) pineapple

1 small, ripe banana

2 tbsp coconut cream

200ml (7fl oz) dairy or soya milk, chilled

a pinch of freshly grated nutmeg

1–2 tsp maple syrup (optional)

a few ice cubes

1 tsp toasted shredded coconut

1 Peel and core the pineapple, then roughly chop and put into a blender. Peel and roughly chop the banana and add to the blender.

2 Spoon in the coconut cream, then pour in the milk and add a pinch of nutmeg. Blend for a few seconds until thick, creamy and smooth. Taste and sweeten with maple syrup if necessary.

3 Pour over ice in two glasses and serve sprinkled with toasted coconut.

Serves 2	EASY	NUTRITIONAL INFORMATION	
	Preparation Time 10 minutes	**Per Serving** 162 calories, 5.8g fat (of which 4.6g saturates), 24.9g carbohydrate, 0.1g salt	Vegetarian • Gluten free

Double Chocolate Velvet

Makes 600ml (1 pint)

2 tbsp chocolate syrup

225ml (8fl oz) low-fat chocolate-flavoured milk, chilled

100ml (3½fl oz) single cream, chilled

2 scoops chocolate ice cream

2 tbsp dark chocolate sauce

1 milk chocolate Flake bar, crushed

a few ice cubes

1 Spoon the syrup into a blender and pour in the chocolate milk and single cream, then add the ice cream. Blend until smooth and well mixed.

2 Divide between two tall glasses and swirl in the chocolate sauce and half the chocolate Flake bar.

3 Top up with ice and serve immediately, sprinkled with the remaining chocolate Flake bar.

EASY	NUTRITIONAL INFORMATION		Serves
Preparation Time 5 minutes	**Per Serving** 515 calories, 30.3g fat (of which 15.3g saturates), 53.6g carbohydrate, 0.4g salt	Vegetarian • Gluten free	**2**

Makes 300ml (¹/₂ pint)

75g (3oz) strawberries

¹/₂ small banana

2 scoops chocolate ice cream

2 scoops vanilla ice cream

a few drops of vanilla extract

125ml (4fl oz) low-fat milk, chilled

1 tbsp low-fat milk powder

1 tsp grated plain chocolate

Neapolitan

1 Remove the hulls from the strawberries, then wash and pat the fruit dry with kitchen paper. Put into a blender and whizz until smooth and thick. Pour into a glass and set aside.

2 Peel and roughly chop the banana and put into a clean blender. Add the chocolate ice cream and blend until smooth and thick. Carefully spoon over the strawberry purée.

3 In a clean blender, blend the vanilla ice cream with the vanilla extract, the milk and milk powder, and then carefully spoon on top of the chocolate layer. Sprinkle with the grated chocolate and serve immediately.

Serves 1	EASY	NUTRITIONAL INFORMATION	
	Preparation Time 10 minutes	**Per Serving** 663 calories, 25g fat (of which 15.7g saturates), 100.6g carbohydrate, 0.6g salt	Vegetarian • Gluten free

Try Something Different

Add a dash of brandy or amaretto liqueur.

Tiramisu

Makes 300ml (¹/₂ pint)

50ml (2fl oz) cold espresso or strong black coffee

75g (3oz) full-fat mascarpone cheese

125ml (4fl oz) full-fat milk, chilled

1 tbsp almond-flavoured syrup or a few drops pure almond essence

1 tbsp maple syrup

1 tbsp whipped cream

¹/₂ tsp drinking chocolate powder

sponge fingers (boudoir biscuits), to serve

1 Pour the coffee into a blender and spoon in the mascarpone. Pour in the milk and add the almond syrup or essence and maple syrup.

2 Blend until smooth and well combined. Transfer to a glass cup and top with whipped cream.

3 Dust with drinking chocolate and serve with sponge fingers to dip.

EASY	NUTRITIONAL INFORMATION		Serves
Preparation Time 5 minutes	**Per Serving** 539 calories, 47.9g fat (of which 29.8g saturates), 21.6g carbohydrate, 0.9g salt	Vegetarian	**1**

5

Party Drinks and Punches

Orange Blossom

Makes 300ml (½ pint)

4 medium oranges

1 lime

a few drops of orange blossom water

1–2 tbsp sugar syrup

a few ice cubes

soda water, chilled

1 Using a sharp knife, cut off the peel from the oranges and lime, removing as much of the white pith as possible. Chop the flesh roughly, discarding any pips, and put into a blender.

2 Add the orange blossom water, then blend until smooth. Taste and add sugar syrup to taste.

3 Divide between two glasses and add a few cubes of ice to each glass. Top up with soda water and serve.

Cook's Tip

To make sugar syrup, put 150g (5oz) granulated sugar in a pan with 275ml (10fl oz) water and set over a gentle heat until dissolved. Bring to the boil and simmer rapidly for 2 minutes. Leave to cool, then use in the recipe. Store the syrup in an airtight container in the fridge. It will keep for up to two weeks.

EASY	NUTRITIONAL INFORMATION		Serves
Preparation Time 5 minutes	**Per Serving** 143 calories, 0.3g fat (of which 0g saturates), 34g carbohydrate, 0.1g salt	Vegetarian Gluten free • Dairy free	**2**

Fruit Planter's Tea Punch

Makes 500ml (18fl oz)

2 cardamom pods

2 tsp good-quality Indian tea leaves

5cm (2in) piece cinnamon stick

2 tsp caster sugar

250g (9oz) mango

150ml (¼ pint) freshly squeezed orange juice or 2 oranges, juiced

a few ice cubes

2 cinnamon sticks to serve

1 Peel the green casing from the cardamom pods and remove the black seeds. Crush the seeds finely using a mortar and pestle.

2 Put the tea leaves into a heatproof jug with the cinnamon, caster sugar and cardamom seeds. Pour in 225ml (8fl oz) boiling water and leave to brew for 5 minutes, then strain through a fine sieve. Allow to cool.

3 Slice the flesh off the central stone of the mango, then peel and chop and put into the blender. Pour in the orange juice and cold tea. Blend until smooth. Pour over ice in two glasses and serve with cinnamon stick stirrers.

Serves 2	EASY		NUTRITIONAL INFORMATION	
	Preparation Time 10 minutes, plus cooling		**Per Serving** 118 calories, 0.4g fat (of which 0.2g saturates), 29.5g carbohydrate, 0g salt	Vegetarian Gluten free • Dairy free

Makes 1.1 litres (2 pints)

200g (7oz) canned pimientos

juice of 1½ lemons

1 medium onion, peeled and chopped

2 tbsp horseradish sauce

1 litre (1¾ pints) tomato juice

2 tsp Worcestershire sauce

1 tsp Tabasco sauce

ground black pepper

175ml (6fl oz) vodka (optional)

finely chopped spring onions to garnish

olives to serve

Spiced Tomato Cocktail

1 Put the pimientos into a blender, add the lemon juice, onion and horseradish sauce, then whizz until blended.

2 Pour into a large jug, gradually add the tomato juice and stir until smooth. Season with the Worcestershire sauce, Tabasco sauce and pepper. Chill until ready to serve.

3 If using vodka, put 25ml (1fl oz) into each glass and top up with the tomato mixture. Garnish with the spring onions and serve with olives.

EASY	NUTRITIONAL INFORMATION	Serves
Preparation Time 10 minutes, plus chilling	**Per Serving** 46 calories, 0.6g fat (of which 0.1g saturates), 9.1g carbohydrate, 1.1g salt Gluten free • Dairy free	**6**

Citrus Gin Sling

Makes 1.1 litres (2 pints)

1½ lemons

3 tbsp golden caster sugar

150ml (¼ pint) freshly squeezed lemon juice

150ml (¼ pint) freshly squeezed lime juice

150ml (¼ pint) gin

ice cubes

soda water

1 Rub half a lemon around the rim of each of six glasses. Put 1 tbsp caster sugar on a saucer and press the rim of each glass into the sugar.

2 Put the lemon and lime juices into a cocktail shaker or screw-topped jar with the remaining sugar and the gin, and shake well.

3 Slice the remaining lemon. Serve the gin sling over ice, topped up with soda water or water to taste. Decorate with a slice of lemon.

Serves 6	EASY	NUTRITIONAL INFORMATION	
	Preparation Time 5 minutes	**Per Serving** 86 calories, 0g fat (of which 0g saturates), 8.6g carbohydrate, 0g salt	Vegetarian Gluten free • Dairy free

Try Something Different

Mango colada: Use a ripe mango instead of the pineapple.

Pina Colada

Makes 400ml (14fl oz)
200g (7oz) pineapple, plus extra to decorate
50g (2oz) fresh coconut
200ml (7fl oz) light coconut milk
200g (7oz) crushed ice
100ml (3½fl oz) white rum

1 Peel and core the pineapple, chop roughly and put into a blender. Roughly chop the fresh coconut and add to the blender.

2 Pour in the coconut milk. Blend until smooth and thick.

3 Transfer to a cocktail shaker, add the ice and rum, and shake for a few seconds to blend and chill. Tip into two glasses, decorate with pineapple and serve.

EASY	NUTRITIONAL INFORMATION	Serves
Preparation Time 5 minutes	**Per Serving** 244 calories, 8.3g fat (of which 6.9g saturates), 15.8g carbohydrate, 0.3g salt Vegetarian Gluten free • Dairy free	**2**

Pineapple and Mint Julep

Makes 600ml (1 pint)

12 mint leaves, plus sprigs to garnish

2 tsp icing sugar

100ml (3½fl oz) bourbon

200g (7oz) pineapple

300g (11oz) crushed ice

2 mint sprigs to decorate

1 Wash the mint leaves and shake dry, then put in the base of a jug. Add the icing sugar and, using a spoon, crush the leaves into the sugar. Pour in the bourbon and set aside.

2 Peel and core the pineapple, then chop roughly and put into a blender. Blend until smooth.

3 Stir the pineapple in with the minted bourbon, then stir in the crushed ice. Divide between two glasses and serve decorated with mint sprigs.

Serves 2	EASY	NUTRITIONAL INFORMATION	
	Preparation Time 10 minutes	**Per Serving** 166 calories, 0.2g fat (of which 0g saturates), 15.3g carbohydrate, 0g salt	Vegetarian Gluten free • Dairy free

Ginger Melon Fizz

Makes 750ml (1¼ pints)

½ orange melon such as cantaloupe or Charantais

1 lemon

2 pieces stem ginger in syrup

a few ice cubes

300ml (½ pint) dry ginger ale, chilled

1 Cut the melon into slices and slice off the skin. Remove the seeds and roughly chop the flesh. Put into a blender. Peel the lemon, removing as much of the white pith as possible. Chop roughly, discarding any pips, and add to the blender.

2 Chop the ginger and put into the blender. Blend for a few seconds until smooth and well blended.

3 Divide between two glasses and add a few ice cubes to each. Top up with dry ginger ale and serve.

Serves 2	EASY	NUTRITIONAL INFORMATION	
	Preparation Time 10 minutes	**Per Serving** 75 calories, 0.2g fat (of which 0g saturates), 18g carbohydrate, 0.2g salt	Vegetarian Gluten free • Dairy free

Cook's Tip

You can leave the egg white out of this recipe but the result will be icier.

Foaming Mixed Berry Sherbet

125g (4oz) strawberries

50g (2oz) raspberries, thawed if frozen, juices reserved

50g (2oz) blackberries, thawed if frozen, juices reserved

50g (2oz) blueberries, thawed if frozen, juices reserved

2 tbsp strawberry syrup

1 medium egg white

6 ice cubes

1 If using fresh berries, hull the strawberries, raspberries and blackberries if necessary. Wash and pat all the fresh fruits dry with kitchen paper, and put into a blender. If the fruit has been frozen, add the juices as well.

2 Add the strawberry syrup and blend for a few seconds until smooth. In a bowl, whisk the egg white until thick and foaming, but not stiff. Transfer to the blender with the ice cubes.

3 Blend for a few seconds until slushy and foaming. Pour into two cups and serve.

EASY	NUTRITIONAL INFORMATION		Serves
Preparation Time 10 minutes	**Per Serving** 86 calories, 0.3g fat (of which 0.1g saturates), 19.1g carbohydrate, 0.2g salt	Vegetarian Gluten free • Dairy free	**2**

Boozy Iced Coffee

Makes 350ml (12fl oz)

125ml (4fl oz) cold espresso or
strong black coffee, chilled

50ml (2fl oz) brandy

50ml (2fl oz) coffee-flavoured liqueur

125ml (4fl oz) single cream, chilled

1–2 tbsp sugar syrup to taste (see Cook's Tip, page 111)

300g (11oz) crushed ice

2 coffee beans, finely crushed

1 Mix the coffee, brandy and coffee liqueur together in a jug. Cover and leave to chill for at least 30 minutes or until ready to serve.

2 Stir in the cream and add sugar syrup to taste.

3 Divide the ice between two tall glasses and pour over the creamy coffee. Serve immediately, sprinkled with crushed coffee beans.

Try Something Different

For a less creamy version, replace the cream with full-fat milk.

EASY	NUTRITIONAL INFORMATION		Serves
Preparation Time 5 minutes, plus 30 minutes chilling	**Per Serving** 272 calories, 12g fat (of which 7.5g saturates), 18.6g carbohydrate, 0.1g salt	Vegetarian • Gluten free	**2**

Try Something Different

Use raspberries instead of strawberries.

Elderflower Cooler

Makes 600ml (1 pint)

225g (8oz) strawberries

2 tbsp elderflower cordial

300ml (½ pint) dry white wine, chilled

a few ice cubes

soda water, chilled (optional)

1 Remove the hulls from the strawberries, then wash and pat the fruit dry with kitchen paper. Put into a blender. Add the elderflower cordial and blend until smooth.

2 Pour into two large glasses and add the wine. Stir and add a few ice cubes to each. Top up with soda water, if you like.

Serves 2	EASY		NUTRITIONAL INFORMATION	
	Preparation Time 5 minutes		**Per Serving** 146 calories, 0.1g fat (of which 0g saturates), 12.1g carbohydrate, 0g salt	Vegetarian Gluten free • Dairy free

Try Something Different

Add 100ml (3½fl oz) rum for an alcoholic punch.

Exotic Fruit Party Punch

Makes 1.1 litres (2 pints)

300g (11oz) pineapple

½ papaya

275g (10oz) mango

2 ripe guavas

2 passion fruit

a few ice cubes

600ml (1 pint) low-calorie lemonade, chilled

1 Peel and core the pineapple, then roughly chop and put into a blender. Peel the papaya and scoop out the black seeds. Roughly chop the flesh and add to the blender.

2 Slice the flesh off the central stone of the mango, then peel and chop and put into the blender. Peel the guavas and discard the seeds if necessary. Chop roughly and add to the blender. Halve the passion fruit and scoop out the seeds and pulp into the blender.

3 Blend until thick and smooth. Transfer to a large jug and add some ice. Carefully top up with lemonade, stirring gently to mix.

EASY	NUTRITIONAL INFORMATION		Serves
Preparation Time 10 minutes	**Per Serving** 117 calories, 0.9g fat (of which 0.1g saturates), 27.1g carbohydrate, 0g salt	Vegetarian Gluten free • Dairy free	**4**

Sea Breeze

Makes 600ml (1 pint)

1 pink grapefruit

125g (4oz) frozen cranberries

100ml (3½ fl oz) vodka, chilled

a few ice cubes

300ml (½ pint) pink lemonade, chilled

1 Using a sharp knife, cut off the peel from the grapefruit, removing as much of the white pith as possible. Chop the flesh roughly, discarding any pips, and put into a blender.

2 Add the frozen cranberries and vodka, and blend until smooth and crushed.

3 Pour into two glasses and add a few ice cubes. Top up with pink lemonade to taste.

Try Something Different

For a simpler version, use 250 ml (9fl oz) grapefruit juice and 100ml (3½fl oz) cranberry juice and stir together with the vodka.

Serves 2	EASY		NUTRITIONAL INFORMATION	
	Preparation Time 5 minutes		**Per Serving** 185 calories, 0.2g fat (of which 0g saturates), 19.7g carbohydrate, 0g salt	Vegetarian Gluten free • Dairy free

Strawberry and Melon Cup

Makes 1.7 litres (3 pints)

300g (11oz) Ogen melon

350g (12oz) strawberries

1.3 litres (2¼ pints) chilled lemonade

450ml (¾ pint) Pimms

ice cubes

sprigs of mint, to decorate

1 Quarter, peel and deseed the melon, then put into a blender and whiz until smooth. Sieve into a large serving jug.

2 Remove the hulls from the strawberries, then wash and pat the fruit dry with kitchen paper. Add to the jug and top up with the lemonade and Pimms.

3 Stir gently, add plenty of ice cubes and decorate with sprigs of mint to serve.

Serves 6	EASY	NUTRITIONAL INFORMATION	
	Preparation Time 10 minutes	**Per Serving** 161 calories, 0.1g fat (of which 0g saturates), 19.9g carbohydrate, 0.1g salt	Vegetarian Gluten free • Dairy free

Index